Fangufangu Mana

Fangufangu Mana

An Awakening to the Gospel in Tonga in the 20th century

Graeme McNae

Fangufangu Mana
Published by Graeme McNae
with Castle Publishing Ltd
New Zealand

© 2024 Graeme McNae

ISBN 978-0-473-69758-7 (Softcover)
ISBN 978-0-473-69759-4 (ePUB)
ISBN 978-0-473-69760-0 (Kindle)

Editing:
Rachel Ross

Production & Typesetting:
Andrew Killick
Castle Publishing Services
www.castlepublishing.co.nz

Cover Design:
Paul Smith

Cover Artwork:
Shea Tagilava

Unless otherwise stated, scripture quotations are from
The Holy Bible, English Standard Version®,
copyright © 2001 by Crossway Bibles,
a publishing ministry of Good News Publishers.
Used by permission. All rights reserved.

See notes at the end of this book for other Bible versions.

ALL RIGHTS RESERVED

No part of this publication may be reproduced,
stored in a retrieval system, or transmitted
in any form or by any means, electronic, mechanical,
photocopying, recording or otherwise,
without prior written permission from the author.

Prologue

A *fangufangu* (nose flute) is a traditional Polynesian musical instrument. When Her Majesty Queen Salote Tupou III reigned in Tonga, it was played by a paramount Tongan chief every morning outside the Royal Palace to awaken her, and to this day its soft tones sound forth from Tonga's national radio station to awaken the whole nation to the new day. One of Tonga's most renowned 19th-century missionaries, Reverend Dr James Egan Moulton, wrote a Tongan language children's morality tale, still familiar with most Tongans, about a young boy who was given a *fangufangu mana*, a supernatural nose flute which, when played, had the power to forbid lies by all reached by its sound. The Good News of Jesus Christ is like a *fangufangu mana*. Those who have ears to hear experience the supernatural power of the gospel through changed lives.

Foreword

In the following pages, you will embark on a remarkable journey alongside a young couple who left their home in New Zealand during the 1970s to serve as Christian missionaries on the beautiful Island of Tonga for a span of fifteen years. Their story is a testament to the profound impact of faith, as they have recounted a multitude of experiences that include surprises, challenges and triumphs. These experiences all point to the incredible work of God in their lives during their time in Tonga, leaving behind a legacy of believers well-equipped to carry forward the message of the gospel after their return to New Zealand. It is a privilege to write this foreword, having known the authors closely as friends during their time in Tonga and continuing that friendship now in New Zealand.

My own journey intersected with theirs in 1978 when I was a senior student at Mailefihi College in Neiafu, Vava'u. I recall listening to a European (*Papālangi*) voice on a Sunday evening radio programme. What piqued my interest was that this *Papālangi* had mastered our language and was able to convey the teachings of the Bible in a way that even a young student like me could understand. Back then, I wasn't particularly focused on scriptures or Christianity. However, when I moved to Tongatapu the following year to attend Tupou High School, my curiosity about God and the Bible grew. I began attending Christian programmes organised by fellow students and became more attentive to radio broadcasts and other Christian gatherings.

One Friday night, a friend invited me to a youth Bible study, and to my surprise, the guest speaker was the same *Papālangi* I had heard on the radio. That was the first time I met Graeme, who was not much older than me at the time. He had his guitar with him and led us in singing Tongan songs before delivering a moving message. I was impressed that he understood our Tongan humour and seemed completely in tune with our culture. This marked the beginning of a lifelong friendship. Over the years, we spent weekends together and kept in touch through phone calls. Reading their story, I gained deeper insight into Graeme and Colleen's journey, discovering many aspects of their experiences that I had not been aware of, particularly the profound, heartfelt challenges that missionaries silently grapple with while navigating life in a foreign land.

Graeme and Colleen's ability to document their journey makes this book a captivating read. Undertaking an overseas mission immediately after getting married and starting a family is a monumental endeavour, especially when it involves learning a new language and comprehending a culture vastly different from one's own to convey the message of faith. They admit to having minimal training for this mission but placed their unwavering trust in God to guide them on their path. Circumstances affirmed their calling to serve, and with the support of local Gospel Fellowships, they embarked on their missionary journey. Their stories illuminate the numerous obstacles and challenges they faced along the way. Yet, they managed to build strong relationships with key figures in the community, providing them with opportunities to share the gospel. What is most fascinating is their success in reaching out to a community and a nation where Christianity had been deeply ingrained for centuries. How do you communicate the gospel to people who have been attending church for their entire lives? How do you convince individuals who claim to be well-versed in the Bible that they need salvation?

Their mission brought them into a unique setting where the church was more tied to culture and tradition than to the spiritual essence of the faith. Many believed that merely belonging to a church and participating in its activities guaranteed their salvation. A particularly intriguing aspect of their journey was the introduction of plural leadership within the church. In Tonga, church leadership is traditionally centred around a single figurehead. Each major church had a sole president at the helm, wielding authority over all members, with the group's success often hinging on the leader's abilities.

However, Graeme and Colleen took a different approach. Elders were appointed under their direction by consensus of the trainee leaders and agreed upon also by the congregation. These elders, including Graeme, jointly lead the church. This decision required local training to help people grasp the benefits and biblical foundation of having multiple leaders within the church. Being in plural church leadership in New Zealand myself, I wish the Tongan churches could practically embrace and foster the benefits and sustainability of plural leadership.

Moreover, because many individuals lacked a deep understanding of the gospel, they were easily drawn to Mormonism. As passionate missionaries, Graeme and Colleen grappled with the crucial question of how to communicate transformational truth to these individuals. During their time in Tonga, they established several fellowships that taught a comprehensive understanding of the gospel, serving as fertile ground for Christians to grow and have a profound impact in the Kingdom. Today, the authors continue to nurture strong connections between these fellowships and sister churches in New Zealand.

I found immense enjoyment in reading Graeme and Colleen's story, not only because I am familiar with the setting but also because I am grateful for the impact they have had on my life.

Growing up surrounded by religious practices, it was by God's grace that I came to understand the essence of the gospel. Tongans and Pacific Islanders will find resonance in this story, but above all, it is a testament to how God can use ordinary individuals to spread the gospel in the mission field.

When we make ourselves available, God provides the resources to make it happen as Jesus reminded us:

> "All authority in heaven and on earth has been given to me. Go therefore and make disciples of all nations, baptising them in the name of the Father and of the Son and of the Holy Spirit, teaching them to observe all that I have commanded you. And behold, I am with you always, to the end of the age." (Matthew 28:18-20)

Professor Palatasa Havea
Massey University
Elder at Church on Vogel, Palmerston North

Contents

Preface		13
1.	The Awakening of Early Servants	19
2.	Stirrings for Tonga in Aotearoa	23
3.	Awakening to the Call	43
4.	Early Challenges	59
5.	The Meeting of the Waters	63
6.	Learning Language and Culture	75
7.	Medical Challenges and Painful Times	83
8.	Starting Foundations	89
9.	Building a Local Church	99
10.	Gospel Living Spreading Wider	109
11.	Women and Children	137
12.	The Word and Witness	145
13.	Open-Air Evangelism	161
14.	The Gospel Sounding to Every Island	171
15.	Man Overboard	175
16.	New Gospel Centres	181
17.	The Senders and the Sent	207
18.	The Pain of Relocation	223
Postscript		227

Appendix 1: The Gospel We Preach	231
Appendix 2: A Legacy	234
Appendix 3: Documents	237
Notes	261

Preface

The story of growing a family in Tonga for nearly two decades is fascinating, but experiencing God at work, planting a church movement amid a society saturated with denominations and cults is quite mind-blowing. Neither my wife Colleen nor I had the credentials expected to make us viable candidates for such a challenge. Ways of negotiating the wide cultural differences were not part of our training or experience. So, being called of God and accepting the challenge is a story we're going to tell. According to the greatest missionary, Apostle Paul, not many mighty are chosen (1 Corinthians 1:26). When it comes to the gospel and its spread throughout the world, all the glory surely belongs to Him alone. Yes, the testimonies of every generation are that all this was God's doing and so it is marvellous in our eyes (Psalm 118:23).

This book is another amazing record of how God visited a religious people a second time to restore the gospel fervour of previous generations. People like John and Charles Wesley and George Whitfield had stirred up a revival amongst a generation consumed with Christian traditions and church practices largely lacking in spiritual fervour. Like the fires in our old homes that needed stoking, or (as Tongans call it) *"tafunaki"*, the church of Jesus Christ needs arousing from generation to generation. The first love grows cold, materialism and an ensuing indifference to Christ replaces evangelism, and the fire of love for God dies down.

Colleen and I have been enriched with the joy of being united with a new culture, a people different from us, who have experienced the wonder of the gospel's transforming power. A Tongan believer's love for Christ is far more emotional, sacrificial and tangible than the European expression we grew up with. We were exposed to new expressions of Christianity as the love of God was spread abroad in their hearts. Over the years, this called for much soul searching, all part of God's unique way of purifying us and making us more fit for the Master's service.

It was Hudson Taylor who challenged people to attempt great things for God and expect great things from God. Our prayer is that this story of His providence and grace will be used to accomplish this in your life, too.

Ko e Fakamālō / Acknowledgements

Kuo 'osi eni ha ta'u e 50 talu 'ema fuofua tu'u 'i Halaleva, Nuku'alofa, 'o kamata ha fononga fakalaumālie mo e kakai ne ui 'e he 'Eikí kiate ia . 'Oku hangē pē ko 'aneafí pea ko e ngaahi manatu melie fau. Ko kinautolu na'a nau fua talitali kimauá, 'oku kei malave 'i homa lotó. 'Oku houngaʻia kiate kimaua 'enau 'ofa u'uu'u 'iate kimaua mo 'ema fānaú, Sioeli, Sānita mo Siini, kae'uma'ā 'a Brent na'e si'i ui foki 'e he 'Eiki 'oku kei valevale.

Ko si'omou faka'atu'i 'ema fu'u solá, na'e lava ke ma 'inasi tetepu ai 'i he ngaahi 'ulungāanga faka-Tonga faka-Kalisitiane. 'E fakangalongata'a 'a kimoutolu, he kuo palotoloto 'iate kimaua 'a e fe'ofa'aki faka-Tongá ko e fe'ofa'aki na'e fakamā'oni'oni'i 'e he Laumālie 'o e 'Otuá tu'unga he ngāue 'iate kimoutolu 'a e Kōsipelí. 'Okú ma fakafeta'i 'i he'etau fāmili 'i he 'Eikí, pea 'e pehē 'o tuputupu'a.

He'ikai lava 'o lau fakalautelau 'a kimoutolu na'e ngaholo ai 'a e ola 'a e Ongoongolelei 'o Sīsū Kalaisí. Ka ko e ki'i ni'ihi pē eni na'a mau kaungāngāue 'i he kamata'angá, ko Setaleki mo Tulaki

Afuhaʻamango naʻá na fua fakanofonofo e ngāué mo ʻofa fakatamaí mo fakafaʻé ʻiate kimaua. Ko Siaosi mo ʻĀlisi Fatafehi naʻá na poupou taʻetuku ʻi he ngaahi feinga kehekehe naʻe faí, pea aʻu ki heʻena luelalo mei Pātangata ki Halaleva ke kau ʻi he ngaahi polokalama kehekehe ʻi falelotu mo tuʻa. Ko Tonga mo Kakala Kātoa naʻá na talitali loto māfana kimaua mo e Ongoongoleleí ki he tofiʻa ʻo Fotú, ki Leimatuʻa.

Ko e toenga ʻo e kiʻi tohi nounou ko ení, ko ha kemo ʻi he fai meʻatoufeiva ʻa e Laumālie Māʻoniʻoní ʻo fanongo ʻa e tokolahi he Fangufangu Mana ʻo e Kōsipelí, ʻa e Ongoongo iviʻia ʻo e ʻOtuá ne fakamoʻui ai ʻa kinautolu naʻe tuí.

Tau kau fakataha ke fakamālōʻia ʻa e Tamai, ʻAlo, mo e Laumālie. Tau kau fakataha mo e kakai ʻo Langi ē, pea faifai pea kau mo māmani fuli pē.

Colleen and I could not have dreamt how much the 15 years in Tonga would bless our family. We owe a debt of thanks to the families of the churches there for the way they embraced us into the Tongan expression of the family of God. All our children were as fluent in Tongan as they were in English – such was their integration into Tongan Christian life – and we are sincerely grateful to God that, in the sphere of the mission, the children experienced a much closer community than they would have back in New Zealand or any other western society.

Without Colleen's total commitment and involvement in every step of the mission we could not have sustained the intensity of the journey.

Our wider family were also an integral part of our mission life. Every member of our immediate family visited and prayed, giving us a deep sense of support even though our visits back to them were few and far between.

We owe Nigel and Melenaite Statham deep thanks for their

comprehensive leading and support as we found our way in the Tongan culture and language. They were most certainly a gift from God to enhance our effectiveness for the gospel.

Deep gratitude is owed to the Brethren churches of New Zealand that sent us out. There are numbers of stories throughout this book that speak of clothing, food parcels and financial gifts sent to us from all parts of the country, Whangarei to Invercargill – such was the love and support of that network of local churches. Many supporters found their way to Tonga as tourists, ensuring that, by accompanying them, we got to spend some days at the beach, and some of these visitors even challenged me on the squash court!

Christian Trusts contributed generously toward the training of Tongan leaders as well as to our own further development through training at Master's Seminary. On our return to reside in New Zealand, the support was extremely generous, allowing us to establish ourselves in the homeland.

It is an undeniable truth that "underneath are everlasting arms" – these arms have been extended from the people of God in Tonga and New Zealand.

For the writing of this book, I owe thanks to Alistair McNaughton and Rob Findlay, who have made great contributions to its structure and readability. Also, thanks to Shea Tagilava for her creative skill in painting the cover and for her interpretation of the *fangufangu*, Tongan nose flute.

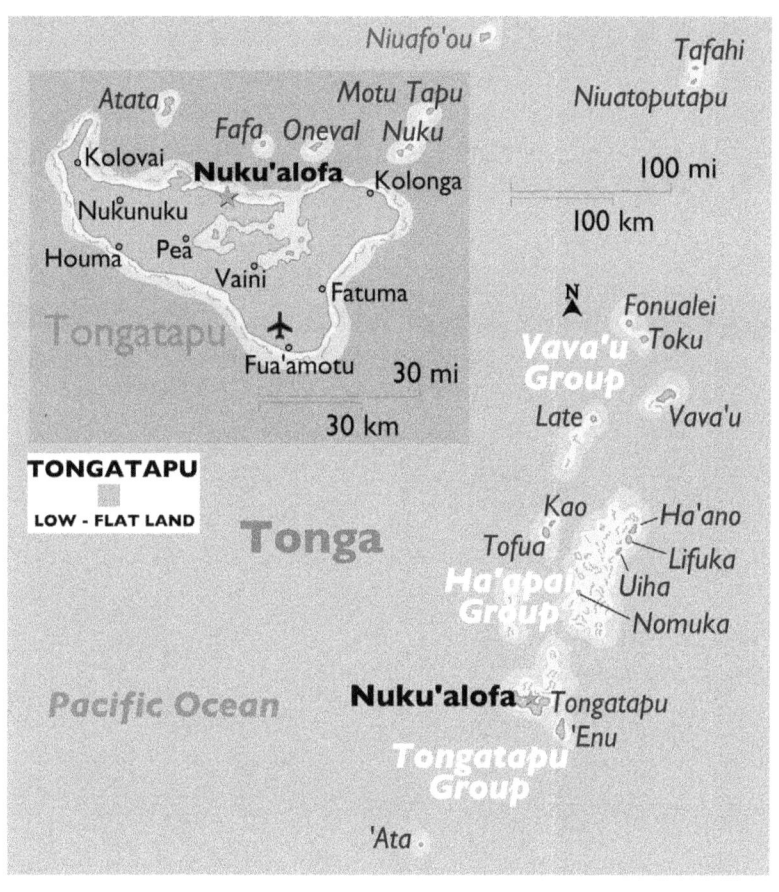

The Kingdom of Tonga, with the main island, Tongatapu, inset. (Map © WorldAtlas.com, used with permission)

Chapter 1

The Awakening of Early Servants

The first evangelical missionaries arrived in Tonga from the London Missionary Society late in the 18th century. Very briefly, ten missionaries arrived on board the *Duff* in April 1797, but by September, having had a level of hospitality from some of the chiefs, a bloody war broke out in which three of them were killed. The others fled and escaped with their lives.

Some 20 years later, in 1822, the Reverend Walter Lawry and his wife Mary arrived on board the *St Michael* from Sydney. They spent their first night on the shores of the large inlet off Muʻa, the original capital of Tongatapu. Only a few kilometres from our home in ʻAnanā. That was September 3, 1822. Difficulties arose between the Tongans and the Lawrys, and more especially with the committee back at mission headquarters in London. Bitterly disappointed, they returned to London in October 1823.

The Lawrys' mission in Tonga has been wonderfully documented by Margaret Reason in *Currency Lass* from the diary entries of Walter Lawry's wife. And one of the best overviews of the spread of the gospel through the Pacific is well-documented in Dr John Hitchen's course, *Roots, Shoots, and Fruit in the Pacific: From Mission Heritage to Pacific Theology*. These two writings, a mere 100 years prior to the one you are about to read, give valuable background for a keen reader looking to gain a deeper perspective of this contemporary story of the gospel being fanned into flame for a second time.

One of the first and most notable Tongan converts to Christianity was Sioeli Pulu (c.1810 – May 7, 1877). His amazing autobiography was printed by the Wesleyan Mission House, London, in 1871 and gives an insight into the work of the Spirit of God on the heart of a Polynesian shaped by idolatry and cannibalism. Pulu wrote,

> When I was a big lad the "lotu" Christianity came to our land. I was full of anger and my soul burned with hatred against it. "And shall our gods be forsaken?" I cried out in great wrath. "As for me I shall never forsake them." There were many also of my mind: and we were one together in our hatred against the lotu, until one day, when we heard of a man talking of it, who said that it promised a land of the dead, different from the Pulotu, land of the dead, of which our fathers spoke – even a home in the sky for the good, while evil men were cast into a dreadful place, wherein there burned a fire which none could quench. On that very night I went forth with our lads of the town. It was a fine night; and looking up to the heavens where the stars were shining, this thought suddenly smote me: "Oh the beautiful land!" If the words be true which were told us today, then these lotu people will be happy; indeed, for I saw the earth was dark and gloomy, while the heavens were clear, and bright with many stars; and my soul longed with a great longing to reach that beautiful land. "I will lotu," I said, "that I may live among the stars." Little did Sioeli realise that not many days hence he would hear of one who died for his sins, one whose name is The Bright and Morning Star, and that he indeed would live with him for ever.[1]

Reverends Cargill and Turner were on Sioeli's island of Vava'u.

A Christian chief, 'Ulukalala, lived there too. The chief prayed for Sioeli, and in so doing, he turned to Christianity, knowing very little of its meaning. From Turner's preaching, Sioeli had heard about sin and the need for repentance, and his heart was heavy with the desire to know what repentance was:

> "Oh what is the repentance whereof the preacher told us?" he cried. "Let me find it that I may live."
>
> At last there came a day (1834) whereon the missionaries assembled to hold a Love-feast... Mr Turner stood up to declare the work of God in his soul. My heart burned within me as I listened to his words; for, in speaking of himself, he told all that I had felt. But while I listened to the words of Mr Turner, my heart was full of joy and love, and the tears streamed down my cheeks. I had previously wept out of sorrow and fear, but now for very joy and gladness, and because my heart was full of love to Him who loved me and gave Himself for me...
>
> "What is this?" the missionaries cried, "What ails you, Sioeli?"
>
> "I live!" I said; "Let me arise, that I may declare the mercies of God." Oh what a day that was! Never can I forget it.[2]

Sioeli served God in Fiji from 1838 until his death in 1877 as a missionary, along with a team of Tongan ministers. These early servants of the gospel, both missionaries and converts, laid a foundation for the spread of Christianity in Tonga and for hearts to be reawakened in the following century.

Chapter 2

Stirrings for Tonga in Aotearoa

A hundred years later, God began stirring a passion for Tonga amongst Christian leaders in Aotearoa New Zealand. The gospel had been growing steadily; however, the need for further leadership, training and direction for Tongan Christians and churches was becoming apparent. The following prominent leaders and missionaries heard the call and visited Tonga during the late 1900s.

Ernie Edwards

Ernie Edwards has a legendary story of evangelistic work amongst the Māori population of Aotearoa, beginning around 1944. However, from as far back as 1955, Ernie expressed an interest in the wider Polynesian community. He wrote,

> For many years some of us have been concerned about the other part of the Māori race in the Pacific Islands. The assemblies known as Open Brethren have, for some reason, practically ignored the South Pacific. A noble work has begun in the Fijian Islands but what of Samoa, Tonga and the Cook Islands and Tahiti?[3]

In the late 1960s, Ernie travelled to Samoa and Tonga, named affectionately by Captain Cook as The Friendly Islands. Aboard the banana boat *Tofua* in July 1962, Ernie traversed many of the

Pacific Islands, eventually arriving on the two main island groups of Tonga, Vava'u in the north and Tongatapu in the south. He spoke passionately about gospel renewal when he wrote:

> If nothing is done within ten years, it appears that the Islands will be largely Mormon, as the Mormon church appears to be prospering and making rapid advances.[4]

Dr Clyde Vautier

Another prominent leader within the Gospel Churches who also had a deep interest in Tonga was Dr Clyde Vautier (25 September 1915 – 26 June 1993) of the Onslow Assembly, Wellington. He played a significant role in establishing the administrative structure of churches, helping with the documentation of a trust made up of New Zealand and developing Tongan leaders. He maintained very close pastoral contact through letters and visits virtually up until the time of his death. Much more will be said about the value of his contributions as this story progresses.

Dr Vautier was a fine Bible Scholar with a double doctorate in Economics and Financial Planning. He was employed by the New Zealand Railways during his time of influence in Tonga. He was a regular preacher at conferences of Gospel Churches in New Zealand, had a significant interest in the development of the Gospel Research Fellowship, and was a founding lecturer at the Bible College in Wellington.

In the late 1960s, Dr Vautier was invited through the New Zealand Government by the Tongan Government to assist in financial planning. Beyond his professional connection with Tonga, he had a personal interest in the spiritual state of the Kingdom. His wife, Kathy, was a direct descendant of the Wesleyan missionary Reverend Walter Lawry, who arrived in Tonga on August 16, 1822.

Walter Lawry was one of the first Wesleyan missionaries from Australia.

During Dr Vautier's term of service to the Tongan Government, he enquired into the state of various churches. He met with the enthusiastic revivalist preacher and Free Wesleyan minister, Reverend Senituli Koloi. They had an intense conversation about the growth of the Scripture Union in Tonga.

The following is a report Dr Vautier wrote in 1969 for the New Zealand Gospel magazine, *The Treasury*, in 1969:

The Kingdom of Tonga

The purpose of my recent visit to Tonga was to survey the position generally, distribute literature, and contact any Christians available. I was assisted by the Director of Education for Tonga (Mr Paul Blomfield) – a true believer – who personally accompanied me to the main secondary schools. Through him, I was able to address some 2,400 senior pupils as well as staff.

My theme was "The Living Word of God – The Book and the Person". After each address – usually through an interpreter – the students were asked to examine various courses in Bible study displayed for the purpose, and then hand into me their names, addresses and requirements. By this means the secondary pupils and a few other adults sent in their names with requests for about 600 courses and supplementary literature. During the evenings I was enabled to give addresses to adults on five or six occasions on scriptural topics.

The literature offered covered the Postal Sunday School Movement range, the Māori Postal Sunday School courses, Emmaus books, Scripture Union courses, and other publications. The amazing thing was the real hunger for the more solid or advanced courses by the older students. Several requests were made for books such as *Guide to Christian Growth*, *Christ loved the Church*, *Messianic Psalms* and the more advanced Māori Postal SS courses. Over 300 wanted PSSM courses and about 100 asked for Māori lessons. Enquiries also for courses for very young children.

One young Tongan lad of 17 confessed personal faith in Christ and said he wanted to learn to be a follower. He had been a pupil for some months at the Suva Gospel Mission School, and, although he had believed secretly, he now made a firm decision. Some serious-minded pupils also asked for Mr Foster Crane's booklet, *The Young Christian*.

At the last address, which was given to about 35 senior pupils of Tonga High School, the head prefect, a girl of 19, came forward and thanked me saying: "I want you to know that everyone in this group is not only a believer, but a true lover of Christ." This was, to some degree, the result of faithful shepherding of a young Tongan woman staff member who had "laboured fervently" in prayer for them. Unfortunately, like the Director of Education there, these active Christians will be shortly leaving Tonga.

Opportunities for Christian Work

The door in Tonga is wide open for Bible literature study courses. Already much valuable work has been done by PSSM. "Joy Bells" is probably the best known publication of its type in the secondary schools. But follow-up work is needed as many past students tend to take on other activities. The new Director of Education has assured me of his preparedness to facilitate the distribution of courses to the various schools and colleges.

However, it seemed to me, the attitude to any new denominations commencing in Tonga is far from favourable. In certain areas this attitude amounts almost, to open hostility.

The people are very religiously minded and ardent church attenders. No work or sport is permitted on Sunday. Church services are arranged for most evenings in the week when lay-reading, choir practice, and sermon preparation courses are given. Even in remote villages you can find the three dominant denominations. The Wesleyan Centennial Church structure is larger than any I have seen in either Australia or New Zealand.

Most churches are conducted on old fashioned orthodox lines, but new and modern ideas are sweeping in. I was privileged to address the entire body of the Free Wesleyan Theological College (Sia'atoutai) and discuss, "the Word" with their lecturers. I rather gather from these discussions and other contacts that the number of true believers in each church is gradually diminishing.

What of the Future of Tonga?
With the recent discovery of evidence of oil deposits, the future of this island Kingdom could change overnight. Today Tonga is an agricultural subsistence economy in which only 11.6 percent are employed and receive wages. There are 80,000 people living in the three main island groups, and of these, 60 percent are under the age of 21. Some 50,000 live on the Island of Tongatapu. 20,000 live in the capital, Nuku'alofa. Tonga is a small country whose natural resources consist of its soil and the surrounding seas and reefs. Its economy is depressed while its population is increasing rapidly. Today, there is a hunger for God's word, but if Tonga was to become materially prosperous, this attitude could change radically.

Could Gospel mission be set up in Tonga? Yes, I think so. Possibly the most likely way would be "two or three" meeting together in a home. Once started, I am sure growth and interest could be rapid. Given one or two believing households established there, results would follow. Living is cheap, and jobs are offered Europeans from time to time in education, agriculture, and such development projects.

Let us pray for Tonga that the Lord may enlarge His work there. Let us pray that hearts may be moved to find employment there to this end. Tonga is New Zealand's nearest neighbour; Tonga is New Zealand's poorest neighbour; Tonga is a neighbour, rich in spiritual potential. Tonga is a real and continuing challenge to us all![5]

Sometime after Dr Vautier's report, he and Ernie Edwards wrote to Foster Crane asking if he would consider visiting Tonga to meet with a small group of Tongans meeting as a free group of Christians under their own leadership. Mr Crane believed these communications from Dr Vautier and Ernie Edwards were the prompting of God's Spirit.

Foster Crane

Dr Vautier's visit to Tonga prompted him to communicate his observations to his long-time missionary friend, Foster Crane, of Fiji. He urged Foster to consider visiting Tonga and make his own assessment. Foster was hard at work establishing churches across Fiji, but eventually, he made the trip.

The following excerpts are a report of that visit made to the Gospel Workers' and Elders' Conference 1971, held in New Zealand:

At the request of a mission organisation Gospel Literature

Outreach and other Gospel Church leaders in NZ I recently spent three weeks in the Tongan Islands with a view to investigating the possibility of furthering Gospel outreach.

It was a challenging assignment for me. The only Tongan I knew was a boy who had attended our Primary School in Suva some years ago. My enquiries too, were limited in that many of the people I endeavoured to contact were unable to speak English.

My first move was to contact a few evangelical leaders (European and Tongan) of the Free Wesleyan Church to sound out their re-actions to a GLO[6] visit – among these was a keen Tongan Minister, Senituli Koloi, a leader of the local Scripture Union Committee. I sat in on one of their committee meetings. Senituli asked me to address a large group of his "lay" preachers on "Baptism and the Sacraments." I agreed to speak provided he let me speak only about the Gospel. We had quite a profitable evening.

To most Tongans, the blessings of God are somehow wrapped up in the "sacraments" of the church and can only be received through the services of Protestant Clergyman, Catholic Priest or Mormon Elders/Bishops.

All of these were sympathetic to a GLO visit, provided literature was confined to the Scriptures, evangelical tracts, Scripture Union notes, etc., and was carried out by the Methodist Youth Fellowships. There was obvious reluctance to the use of any literature relating to baptism and the church, or that may upset the status quo of the Free Wesleyan Church.

Another of the groups I wanted to meet with was a small group of believers in Nukuʻalofa known as the "Fanga Fellowship." (Fanga is the name of a local suburb in Nukuʻalofa).

The history of the Fellowship is briefly as follows. About

six years ago in the Vavaʻu Group (160 miles to the north) two men, Fine Taue and Setaleki Afuhaʻamango were saved and baptised through the witness of a passing Evangelist from Pangopango in American Samoa.

Not knowing what church to join, Fine and Setaleki commenced a work of their own in Vavaʻu calling it the "Neiafu Baptist Fellowship" simply because they practiced believers' baptism. (They assure me they have no connection with Baptists as such, though, along with other visitors, one or two Baptists had visited them). Both men continued to support themselves but declared that their main object in life is to "preach the Gospel in the darkness."

Fine and Setaleki moved to Nukuʻalofa and rented a place for meetings but, owing to their extreme poverty, they could not pay the rent and had to give it up. They moved to another place but met with much opposition from the established churches so returned to Vavaʻu. In 1970 they returned to the Capital, Nukuʻalofa, and made another start holding meetings in Seta's house – a small 20′ × 15′ room that was very run down. They dropped the word "Baptist" and simply called themselves the "Fanga Fellowship".

I had the names of these two men on my list and, remarkably enough, I met Seta on the waterfront the first day I arrived and had a long talk with him. He told me about the Fellowship and asked me to speak at it on Sunday night. I agreed. It was not until later when checking my list that I discovered that this was the "key" man I had been asked to contact!

About 50 adults and children managed to find seating (on the floor) in the small room. Most of these were visitors.

Fine opened the meeting and he was followed by a local elder, who gave a short talk. Because of the poverty there were only two hymn books so Fine read each verse before it was sung. The singing was quite fantastic, deep, natural harmony which filled the small room.

I then spoke by interpretation, after which the Fellowship Members took the Lord's Supper. This was passed around by Fine to the members who simply knelt where they were in the congregation: the bread was cut in pieces and separate cups used (real wine). The supper is observed once a month. Finally the meeting was opened for prayer in which Seta's wife took part. All present were then invited to a typical meal prepared each Sunday night by Seta and his wife, and that out of their extreme poverty. They apologised (to me) for the fact that they possessed only one spoon and knife for the whole family of nine children: as guest of honour, I was given first use of the spoon and it was then passed round to others who wished to eat with it!

Some aspects of their church activities, I found unusual and, to some extent unscriptural. But having had no contact with outside evangelical Christians or assembly practices, it was perhaps to be expected that they would carry on the practices with which they were previously familiar.

Against this, however, were three clear desires on their part –

(a) To meet on a strictly non-denominational basis recognising only true believers as members of the church of God, avoiding any name that may suggest they were forming a new denomination.

(b) To preach the Gospel of the grace of God. They have meetings in homes or open-air on weeknights which may continue till midnight. As they have no transport, members must walk long distances.

(c) To baptise converts by immersion. Five were baptised

in the sea (by Fine) while I was with them – four men and a young married woman – and I have never seen a baptism carried out in a more dignified and gracious manner: the dear girl walked slowly from the sea singing quietly to herself with tears rolling down her face. I do not think there was a dry eye in the whole group.

After the Gospel meeting referred to earlier, the Fellowship members asked if I would discuss with them their main problem – the need of a more suitable meeting place; it was obvious that their witness could never make much progress in Seta's collapsing house. One of their adherents had offered to let them have a block of three acres in quite a good locality in a suburb of Nuku'alofa on condition that they gave him a boat! They had, in fact, accepted his offer and had commenced clearing the land of bush.

At their request I later went to see the land and watched the women weaving coconut leaves for the walls of a temporary meeting place, the men were clearing trees and planting taro and yams. I discussed the purchase conditions with Sefo (the owner) and the elders, but as nobody had any idea as to the type of boat Sefo wanted, I advised him to set a price and this he eventually did at $2,400.

Unlike all outside missions who pour tens of thousands of dollars into the country, the believers had no outside contacts and were practically cent less. It says something for their courage that they had commenced clearing the land without the faintest idea of where the money was to come from. They had some vague hope that some of their members may be able to go to New Zealand to earn money.

Was it a coincidence that on the evening of this discussion I read almost casually in Ezra 6:8 "I make a decree what ye shall do to the elders of these Jews, for the building of this house of God; that of the King's goods even of the tribute beyond the river forthwith expenses be given unto these men that they be not hindered." (KJV)

After a trip to Vavaʻu, I was due to return to Suva however the elders, wanted further discussion with me, so they came together the same night at 1 a.m. and we continued our talk till 3.30 a.m. – five of us sitting on the floor of Seta's house around a smoky kerosene light, my head reeling! I did not feel I could leave them in their tangle, so cancelled my flight for several days.

I could no longer avoid the fact that I had to make a decision – either we support these people, or we don't. I was greatly burdened with the responsibility that weighed upon me, and just longed for another responsible brother with whom to consult – but there was none. I was not altogether happy about their activities and was a little fearful of the "risk" involved.

Against this, however, three important factors were apparent.

1. The remarkable way in which the Lord appeared to be leading – the prayers of Gospel Churches in NZ – my unexpected meeting with Seta the day I arrived – my sudden appearance into the fellowship group almost the very day they were facing a land problem. They looked upon me as a direct answer to their prayers – an "angel" from God who had, almost literally dropped into their midst from Heaven. Who was I to resist the work of God? If it was His doing, could He not care for the future?

2. The fact that this was a wholly indigenous move from within the country. Any attempt to establish assembly

work from without would almost certainly, have met with Government refusal. It was a very definite crack in the wall, that may never open a second time.

3. It was a clear answer to the GLO problem – a definite permanent centre of activity within the country from which the Gospel may radiate, and literature be distributed, without any compromise to Biblical truth. Guides and interpreters are available. The Fellowship is most happy to welcome visitors from overseas, and has agreed that 2 permanent rooms be added to the proposed meeting-house for workers.

With all these things in mind I told the Solicitor that I – "we" would accept responsibility for the initial payment.

On the final Sunday night, I met with the Fellowship again, and we endeavoured to get the work on a more stable footing, and adopt a plan. It was agreed –

(a) To recognise a definite eldership of the fellowship.

(b) To call the new development the "Halaleva Gospel Fellowship" – their suggestion – Halaleva is the name of the district. Trustees were appointed and a simple constitution prepared.

(c) To open a Bank account under the same name.

(d) To erect a new meeting place of 40 feet by 20 feet, with adjoining rooms for visitors as the Lord enables.

For the benefit of our assemblies overseas, I suggest the following –

1. Establish a "Tonga Development Fund" in Suva, with the object of assisting in the land purchase, the building

programme, the provision of Tongan literature, local workers, subsidies to Tongans attending our proposed Bible School in Suva, and related activities.

2. Assist a couple of single Māori young men with a knowledge of carpentry – or a married man with his wife to go to Tonga and help with the building. They should be able to give spiritual help and counsel also. This is quite an urgent matter. The Fellowship will provide immediate accommodation – Tongan fashion. Visitors permits are available for six months. I have application forms for any who are exercised. I suggest Māori workers on account of their racial kinship with Tongans. The presence of Europeans is inclined to create the impression that a new "Papalagi" (white man's) denomination is being established.

3. With the completion of the building a Māori evangelist could hold a campaign.

4. Two or three GLO workers (Māori preferably) could follow this over a further six-month period.

5. Visiting Bible teachers – possibly our own local Fiji workers – could pay occasional visits. The Fellowship needs a great deal of instruction concerning Local Church order and practice, but I feel they are willing to learn.

6. Keen Tongan Christians could be encouraged and assisted to attend the Bible School in Suva for three months. Several are already interested, but practically all expenses would have to be paid by us. The future development of the work will largely depend on these latter young people.

We commend this work to your prayerful and practical fellowship.[7]

Each of these three – Edwards, Vautier and Crane – were held in high regard among the Gospel Assemblies in New Zealand. They each had significant experience in mission, particularly with Pacific Island people. Their involvement in the vision to reach Tonga would have been supported by many churches, along with sincere and earnest prayer for a positive outcome.

Dr Victor Wilson

The fourth foreign supporter to be involved in this formative stage was already living in Tonga as a volunteer. By God's providence, Dr Victor Wilson arrived as a V.S.A. (Volunteer Service Abroad) in March of 1972. V.S.A was a charitable organisation established by Sir Edmund Hillary in 1962 and has maintained its contributions to Tonga until the present day. Dr Wilson was assisting in the field of agriculture. He was a committed Christian and a good friend of Dr Vautier, and he enthusiastically engaged with this small Christian group. From original documents, we have been provided with invaluable information and insights regarding the organisational development of the Tonga Gospel Fellowship. As a meticulous note-keeper, Wilson has left us some thirty pages of handwritten minutes in which he recorded discussions and decisions over two years (1972-1973). The following is a sample of his records.

This is the first official report of the Tonga Gospel Fellowship:

Chairman's Annual Report. 26 June 1973.

Dear Brothers and Sisters in Christ,

It has been an honour and a privilege to serve the Lord as your Chairman, Secretary and Treasurer for the past year. When I arrived in Tonga in March 1972, I was a complete stranger, yet because I had been redeemed by the blood of the Lord Jesus Christ you all welcomed me with open arms and we have worked together for the Lord ever since.

Although it is very unusual for one person to act in three capacities, yet, because of circumstances, it was felt that by this method, one could show the Fellowship as quickly as possible, some of the basics of looking after the business side of the Fellowship.

I consider we all have made considerable progress during this past year and now the Christians of the Fellowship are better able to take their place as a group of Christians in the community life of Tonga and will be better able to serve the Lord Jesus Christ.

Held in Setaleki's house, Halaleva, on 26 June 1973. 9.00 p.m.[8]

Dr Wilson also presented a simple statement of faith to the leaders as an attempt to offer principles for the church to build on. This was a note written into the minutes of a church meeting.

Statement of Faith

The Bible is the inspired Word of God.
The Lord Jesus Christ God/man; died as a sacrifice for sins.
He rose again physically and will return in last days.
Salvation is by faith in the Lord Jesus Christ.

The Church.
    Made up of believers only.
    All members to be baptised by immersion.
    Each group should meet with fellow Christians in each locality as local interdenominational churches.[9]

There was no discussion recorded of these principles, nor a translation. The small congregation would have had very little understanding of the importance of such a statement.

Throughout 1972-1973, the small group established an official identity within Tonga under the name Tonga Gospel Fellowship. A plot of land was registered, and a building for worship was constructed with finances primarily from New Zealand and labour from families of the fellowship. A sample of one of these meetings, along with photocopies, have been printed in the indices to establish the authenticity of this record.

Following Foster Crane's visit in 1972, a group of young people in the church were selected to attend Coral Coast Bible School in Fiji. They included Ofa Fatafehi, Saia Unufe, Paula and Vaisioa Afuha'amango, Limi Hai and Samiuela Tukipili.

Foster Crane and Dr Vautier jointly decided to seek assistance from New Zealand Gospel churches to build a meeting place for this group and establish Gospel churches in Tonga. The minutes Dr Wilson kept indicated that he, together with Setaleki and his relationship with some of the nobility proved to be a formidable combination in having the church recognised and approved by government. In the later stages of 1972, Setaleki negotiated with a landowner, Sio, to purchase land in Halaleva. Subsequently, the plot of land was surveyed and registered in the name of Tonga Gospel Fellowship, with one lot designated for religious purposes and the second for residential purposes. The land was leased from the Crown for 50 years. Copies of those documents are in the indices. Setaleki reported that King Taufa'ahau IV regarded this as the last new denomination that would be registered in Tonga.

Providentially again, a builder from New Zealand, Bernie Tolmie, offered to come to Tonga and take responsibility for the construction. He arrived in January 1973.

The first church building on Halaivahamama'o Road (Bypass

Road), a district known as Halaleva, was completed in December 1973. One of the most significant issues the group needed to resolve was the involvement of government dignitaries at an opening ceremony. Inviting nobility or royalty to such an event would give the new church mission a degree of national respectability and recognition; however, it would also require significant cultural procedures, which would come at considerable cost to such a small group. Some of the group wanted the King to dedicate the building, thereby sanctioning his approval of this new denomination. In the minutes of two successive meetings, Dr Wilson made the following notes:

> **Meeting of 21st September**
> As Paula Tupou leaves for Vava'u at the end of the month the question of who should open the Chapel was discussed. Much discussion took place on inviting His Majesty the King of Tonga, but when this was put to the vote the motion was lost by one vote. Some members contended that they were not clear as to what they were voting for, therefore the chairman allowed another vote to be taken.
>
> This time the voting was reversed and the motion was carried by one vote. After Bernie Tolmie had spoken, some members stated that they were still confused.
>
> The chairman then explained that the resolution was carried, but in view of the lack of notice of the extraordinary meeting, and the approximate equal voting in both cases, he considered another meeting should be called in a week's time and would do so if asked to do by two or more members.[10]
>
> **Meeting of 30th September**
> After Tu'ulaki Afuha'amango, Paula Tupou and Bernie Tolmie had all spoken at length on the pros and cons of the

involvement of royalty at the opening of the Chapel, it was finally moved by the chairman and seconded by Tuʻulaki and Fatulisi jointly, that when the date is finally decided to open the Chapel, Mr Foster Crane and Dr Clyde Vautier be invited to attend and conduct an opening ceremony of Prayer and Praise and spiritual edification. This was carried unanimously.

Notably, neither Setaleki, Siaosi nor Fine, senior members of the group, were at this second meeting. The decision not to involve the King may well have been a watershed moment that placed the centrepiece of church organisation around spiritual priorities rather than cultural expediency, building solely on the Gospel foundation, Jesus Christ, as opposed to aligning with political or even denominational influences; the humility and sacrifice that Jesus taught, rather than the pomp, power and influence of earthly authorities. Tongan society, being hierarchical, has encountered much controversy and factions in its church polity that has muddied the waters of church leadership principles as taught in scripture:

"You know that the rulers of the Gentiles lord it over them. It shall not be so among you," Jesus said. (Matthew 20:25)

He [Jesus Christ] has put all things in subjection under His feet, and gave Him as head over all things to the church, which is His body, the fullness of Him who fills all in all. (Ephesians 1:22, 23 NET)

Similarly, Paul encountered these leadership problems in Corinth as the members aligned themselves with either Apollos, Peter or Paul (1 Corinthians 1).

During these early meetings, under Dr Wilson's guidance, a simple constitution was drafted and accepted. Also, throughout this building time, Foster had begun establishing a biblical foundation of truth in the lives of the five sent by the church to the Bible school. One was 'Ofa Fatafehi, son of Siaosi and Alisi Fatafehi. 'Ofa's story is an example of a new generation of disciples of Jesus that God used to establish and grow the fellowship in Tonga – a wider story that will be told in greater detail as this book unfolds.

Chapter 3

Awakening to the Call

Long before these connections were woven together towards establishing an evangelical mission into Tonga, Colleen and I (Graeme) were being woken to the call of God, preparing us for our life's journey.

Colleen had been born into a strong evangelical home and faithfully nurtured into a sound faith. Ces Hilton, her dad, was known throughout New Zealand as a passionate Irish evangelist and, along with his wife Mavis, had impacted thousands with the gospel, directing large numbers of these to local assemblies of Christians.

Colleen's mother, Mavis, was a true discipler in the home. Their four children, Russ, Jenny, Colleen and Torrey, witnessed her dedication to her husband and the cause of Christ. In what better environment could one be brought up in preparation for mission?

Colleen had come to a simple yet genuine faith as a child under her mother's influence. She completed secondary school in 1969 and started training as an Occupational Therapist in Rotorua Hospital. But in 1970, she took significant time out to attend the Assembly Bible School in New Lynn, Auckland, to further her Christian training.

My parents, too, shaped my life toward the mission of Christ. They had played a significant role in the life of Te Kuiti Assembly since 1953. In those days, Te Kuiti Assembly was thriving, with at least ten or more families making up a vibrant community of real salt-of-the-earth people. Among the most influential of these were Tom and Shirley Walsh, Edmond and Miriam Whitelock, Edith and Horace McCann, Pip and Ruth Parker, Bob and Ruth Jackson, Ken and Pat Allen, Mr Christensen, Vera Kapoor and her children, Marion, John and George White, Bob and Cicely Geange, Ruth Johnston, Phil and Eunice Duxfield, Merv and Avis Nelson and Reg and Margret Pask. Along with their children, over 30 in total, the weekly Sunday School and Bible classes played a formative role in these families' spiritual development, particularly for me. Surely this speaks to the value of sound Bible teaching and a vibrant community experience for families. Remarkably, this has been repeated in the Tongan churches, which we will presently discover.

So, one of my earliest memories of spiritual awakening came during the singing of the well-known hymn one Sunday afternoon in Bible study:

Follow, follow, I will follow Jesus.
Anywhere, everywhere I will follow on.[11]

I remember the day vividly. It was as if God was planting a seed in a child to be willing to go wherever He might send.

Since my father was the church secretary, we often hosted visiting missionaries and itinerant Bible teachers from around the world, including India, South America, China and, of course, the South Pacific.

One visitor was Foster Crane, a close relative. He was married to my mother's sister, Gwen, so the family, including their children, Joanna and Arthur, often spent extended time on our Otorohanga farm as they travelled around New Zealand on mission deputation.

I clearly remember another mission-inspiring moment while barely a teenager. I overheard a conversation my parents were having around the topic of mission. Foster commented that he could think of no greater honour that could come to parents than having one of their children commit to serving God in the environment of another culture. I had no idea what cross-cultural mission was, but for some reason, that moment remained in my consciousness right up until the time of God's call some ten or more years later.

But before any thought of mission had entered my innocent, young mind, there needed to be a personal meeting between the Saviour and my sinful heart.

In August of 1957, my older brother, Murray, invited Peter (my twin) and I to travel with him to Marton and attend a boys' camp at the Marton Children's Home. Children from the Every Boy's Rally[12] programme would gather for one week during the school holidays.

"Uncle" Bernie Holmes gathered a team around him and gave us a wonderful week of fun and learning Bible truth. On one of the last nights of camp, Mr Alf Chote, a missionary home on furlough from India, gave a talk that caught my attention. Jesus Christ, God's Son, had died for me. That was the first time I remember hearing of and processing the personal love of Jesus Christ for me.

Uncle Bernie made a simple but clear invitation for anyone who would like to accept the forgiveness of Jesus Christ offered through His death on the Cross to come and talk to him.

The programme closed, so while the boys were milling around the servery for their cup of hot milo, I went rather shyly to Uncle Bernie.

At that moment, he was rolling up an electric cable around his arm following the movie we had watched.

"I'd like to become a Christian," I said, looking up at this tall, gentle giant.

"Do you want to pray now, or would you like to come to my room?" he said.

"Right here, now, will be fine," was my response. I have no

memory of what I prayed, but what followed was evidence enough that God had renewed my heart. Amazing!

The boys had all gone off to their bunks for the night. Pete was in a top bunk above mine, so I climbed up the ladder and said,

"Hey Pete, are you a Christian?" Pete was a bit stunned at the out-of-the-blue question. He didn't know what to say!

"I've just asked Jesus Christ into my life. You should do the same," I continued.

We took the long journey back to the King Country in an old steam train a few days later. Dad met us at Te Kuiti station. As soon as we arrived home, I ran into Mum's room. She was still waking up as it was only about 6.00 a.m.

"Mum, guess what happened at camp?"

"What?" she said, giving me a big mama hug.

"I became a Christian; I asked Jesus Christ into my life."

She seemed delighted.

I was still young, so I didn't seem to make much progress as a Christian. But regular attendance at Sunday School in Te Kuiti, and the friendships I made had a solid impact at that stage of my life.

A couple of years later, Billy Graham, the renowned international evangelist, was touring New Zealand and Australia, preaching to tens of thousands in large venues like Carlaw Park in Auckland. Provincial towns, like Otorohanga, were connected via a telephone landline where churches combined into large public halls to hear a live broadcast of the gospel from the main centres. That was a night to remember, as I publicly confessed faith in Jesus Christ by responding to an appeal to go forward for counselling.

I made a relatively weak move to become more serious about my faith by being baptised. However, the teenage years challenged my commitment to Christ. Rugby, an awareness of girls, and an introduction to the party life associated with sport affected my spiritual growth. I became a hypocrite and knew it.

But God promises to bring to completion what he begins (Philippians 1:6), and there was another significant moment to come. In my final year of school, 1967, while on an exchange tour playing rugby and basketball in Gore, I was confronted by my closest friends. I had a profession of being a Christian but a lifestyle that didn't match it.

"He's a church attender, but basically, he's just the same as us," said a girl who knew me well.

Wow, that stung me. I felt ashamed! Nothing life-changing happened until a year later. I left school and home, about to enter the big wide world alone.

As I was preparing to start work in Nelson, my older brother invited me to go to the Mount Maunganui Bible Class camp for ten days and help with the cooking for 1,500 people. My job was to peel 15 sacks of potatoes each morning and clean the huge pile of cooks' dishes and dirty pots after each meal. But I also had a secret motivation. Was there a pretty girl I could check out and befriend? And there was! That's where I first met Colleen Hilton, daughter of a well-known evangelist. We were mutually attracted, so when I returned to Otorohanga briefly and told my parents of the emerging friendship, they made it clear that I would have to clean up my act if the friendship was to continue.

"Huh," I thought. I was slightly offended by their convicting comments, but God was about to start a major overhaul, as He does.

I travelled by train to Wellington and flew across to Nelson on a DC3. Finding my way to 41 Brunner St, where Jim and Beulah Pinkerton had kindly offered to give me a room in their home, I was shown my room, entered, and shut the door. As I was about to unpack my small suitcase, what I can only describe as a real sense of the presence of God's Spirit came over me. I was about to begin a new life independent of my parents and anyone who knew anything about my past. It was as if God spoke into my heart.

"You've been mine for some years but ashamed of Me."

I suddenly faced up to the double life I'd been living. It was time to get real with God. I dropped to my knees beside the bed, saying, "Lord, I'm sorry. I'm coming home. I want my life to be all yours."

That was the moment I truly reengaged with Jesus Christ and His Lordship. And as they say, the rest is His story. Amazing mercy, amazing grace!

A matter of weeks after this major turnaround, my decision to follow Christ was rechallenged. This time in my sporting world, which I loved. A friend at work asked if I would like to be on the reserves for a game of rugby for a club in Stoke, just out of Nelson. No harm in that, I thought. So, I played the game and did well. The coach then pressed me seriously to join the club. It so happened that the week before, at church, one of my new friends told me, "If ever you've got a question about your life and you want to talk, just give me a call."

When asked to join the rugby club, I hesitated. I should call my friend, Uncle Sid, and see what he thought. We arranged a lunch hour in the Queen's Gardens in Nelson.

"So what's on your mind?" he said.

I told him of my query regarding playing rugby.

His response was pointed and powerful: "Graeme, what do you want to do with your life?"

Well, that was direct! "I'm interested in mission," I said, "but basically, I want to live for Jesus Christ."

"So, what do you think about rugby?" he queried.

It was another life-changing moment. No to rugby, yes to Christ.

In 1968, I started my job in the government's Department of Scientific and Industrial Research (DSIR) in the Entomology Section as a Science Technician.

The Gospel Church on Rutherford Street provided an excellent and nurturing environment for my new-found faith, giving me an example of a healthy, functioning church ideally suited for my spiritual growth. There were at least five families with teen-aged children – the Greenfields, Cedermans, Dimocks, Packers, Shirtliffs, Baynes and Hockeys, so plenty of scope for youth activities and the development of evangelistic/discipleship programmes.

The Nelson District had several thriving churches in Stoke, Richmond, Hope and Tasman that were mutually supportive, each with vibrant evangelistic and mission ministries.

On one memorable occasion, God focused my attention on mission. Our church visited the Hope Community Church for special services with an Australian missionary/preacher, Colin Tilsley. At the close of the Sunday evening service, he invited any who wanted to respond to God's appeal for missionaries to make themselves available to go to any country. I was deeply moved by that challenge and, without anyone knowing, since I was sitting in the back, rose to my feet to indicate, "Here am I, Lord, send me."

Throughout this time, Colleen and I were developing a relationship that would turn into a lifetime commitment. Most of it was done through what's now called "snail mail", anything up to three letters a week. During those long-term, written conversations, we refined our goals for married life and the priority we'd give to God's Word and will. That long gestation period lasted around four years, putting us in good stead for the tough years ahead. Together, we offered our relationship to God, agreeing that if a mission call came for us to go overseas, we'd be available.

We were married in 1971 and settled in Nelson. Discussions around evangelism and overseas mission were a regular part of our conversations, but when and how was all a mystery. We dove into the church life, reaching out to the youth community through a weekend coffee bar event. We had plenty of experiences discipling new Christians under the tutelage of great leaders. I was learning how to teach and preach in the main church sessions. It was like a Christian form of apprenticeship – in-service training. This was all invaluable for what we were about to embark on.

In 1972, the DSIR underwent a restructuring phase whereby the Nelson centre closed. Staff were given the choice of relocating to either Auckland or Christchurch. Was this the turning point we'd been waiting for? What did relocation mean for us? How could we know God's will? Move to Auckland or Christchurch or...?

Routine prayer and daily Bible reading became a much more purposeful part of our lives. We had a deep desire to further our knowledge of scripture and become involved in mission work of some sort. Colleen's father had set up a Bible College at Kaitoke, Upper Hutt. Was that an option? I was slightly averse to taking an easy route and attending a family-run school.

One morning in March 1973, I was reading the of experience of Elijah and his prediction of judgement from God on Ahab for allowing Baal worship in Israel and marrying the wicked Jezebel. Drought would cripple them. I was flying down a steep hill off Britannia Heights on my bike when the verses in 1 Kings gripped me:

> "Get thee hence from here and go East and camp by the brook Cherith... I've commanded the ravens to feed you there." (1 Kings 17:2-4 KJV)

It was almost like a premonition. Where's east from here? Check the map. East from Nelson is slightly north of Upper Hutt. *What!* It was as if God was saying to me, "There's a brook, a small creek there, and your provisions will be provided from an outside source since the move will require resigning from paid employment."

We discussed this experience together and within a few days had made the decision. This was the Lord's leading! In hindsight, I'd have to say if we're looking for God's guidance, this is not exactly how to go about it. We should not read the Bible looking for statements that seem to fit our own plans. On the other hand, reading and meditating on the scriptures is how God has led his people down through the ages. Be that as it may, in our infancy of walking in God's ways, the subsequent events confirmed it was indeed the Lord impressing on us our need to change direction from employment and learn to trust him, all in preparation for the next steps.

So, with DSIR restructuring and relocating, I took this opportunity to accept neither alternative but rather resign from DSIR and attend a Bible College in Kaitoke to further our preparation for mission. When I advised the head of the department of this decision, Dr Peter Fenemore was shocked.

He said, "You're a young man with a young family, leaving a great career to attend a Bible School?! You're a fool. You're throwing your life away."

To which I replied, "Sir, two thousand years ago, Jesus Christ gave his life away for me. I could do nothing better than to lay down mine for him."

Well, it was one thing to move everything we owned (not much) to Kaitoke, Upper Hutt, but the course was only for six months. Then what? During the course, we were uncertain of our future, so decided to write to Foster Crane and ask if he had any prayer items relating to mission in the South Pacific. We were oblivious to the visits he had made to Tonga and the decisions that had been made regarding a building.

He replied quite quickly, giving us the names of the four Tongan lads studying at Coral Coast Bible School, Fiji. He suggested we pray for God to raise up people to shepherd them in Tonga and help them become established as Christians. He made no mention of his recent involvement with the small group in Tonga.

"Great!" we thought. So we began praying earnestly for God to raise up someone to nurture these young students in Tonga.

After a week or so, Colleen asked a very poignant question: "Would we be willing to answer our own prayer?"

I recall answering her in a rather demeaning tone, "We're barely in our 20s. How could we do something that challenging?"

To which she replied, "We don't need to assume it is us, but rather tell God of our willingness and availability!"

"Ok then, let's do that," I said.

So, we took the next step and told the Lord of our willingness to go if He chose. We distinctly remember offering ourselves to God despite our obvious lack of training or experience. Ever heard God's requirement, not ability but availability?

Through praying, we became more serious about helping in Tonga. The next question was, how would we know for sure that it was His will for us? Just a few weeks later, we noticed an invitation to a Polynesian workers' hui on a marae in Auckland on the Bible School notice board. We decided to leave young baby Joel with family and travel up to Henderson. Arriving, we parked the car and walked the footpath towards the entrance. Coincidentally, another person was walking in the same direction. Noticing he appeared to be a Polynesian, I asked where he was going.

"Oh, to a conference on South Pacific Mission at this marae right here."

Taken aback, I said, "So where are you from?"

"Tonga," he said!

Can you believe it? We'd travelled seven hours to attend a Polynesian workers' conference, thinking all the while about Tonga. Here we were at a conference and totally out of our comfort zone! My heart skipped a beat. The first random person we met before the conference even started was a Tongan! Coincidence or providence, random or design? And he was the only Tongan at the conference! There began a lifelong friendship with Kelepi Mailau, a foundation leader of the Navigators, a discipleship movement in the process of establishment in Tonga.

While at Kaitoke Bible School, we had decided to make enquiries with Tonga Immigration for a visa to reside in Tonga for mission purposes. Within a few weeks, we had a response saying clearly that we would only be given a three-week visitors' visa. This was a knockback. We decided to confide in Mr Gordon Junk, the Principal of the College. He invited us into his office and asked for the letter. He said, "As Hezekiah did in Isaiah 37, we will spread this letter before the Lord." So he did, and we prayed that God would overrule in a sovereign way and allow us to get a residency visa. The sequel to this prayer will come a little later in the story.

Still unsure whether or not we should go to Tonga, I asked God, "Please give us some promise from Scripture as a confirmation." It happened one morning a few weeks later, in Mount Maunganui, during a Bible School mission project. I was having my personal devotions reading through Ephesians, and off the page jumped these words:

> Therefore be imitators of God, as beloved children. And walk in love, as Christ loved us and gave himself up for us, a fragrant offering and sacrifice to God. (Ephesians 5:1,2)

The challenge was clear. Could I, would I, offer up my life for the sake of the gospel for Tonga? Sacrifice home and family for the Tongan people for the sake of the Good News of God's grace through Jesus Christ?

"It's a 'yes' from me," I said.

After an emotional time praying, I ran to tell Colleen. Together we agreed this was the confirmation we'd been waiting for. It remains a landmark in our lives: May 1973.

The call to mission was given by Jesus in His Great Commission in Matthew 28:19,20. But this specific call to a cross-cultural mission had to be more than two individuals making their own independent decision. We believed strongly in the importance of a local church leadership commendation to ratify or confirm the validity of the call.

We visited the elders of our home church, Rutherford St, Nelson. When we explained the background and the journey to what we felt was God's call, the eldership's response was confirmation and encouragement. The elders said they had been expecting something like this for some time. They had seen the involvement in church life, the training we willingly participated in and the harmony we had with the church-affirming qualities. Colleen's home church in Fenton Park, Rotorua, endorsed the commendation. Soon afterwards, acknowledgement was published in the national magazine, *The Treasury*, that we were being commended to mission work in Tonga. It was official.

As it happened, one of the lecturers at Kaitoke Bible School was Dr Clyde Vautier. He took a particular interest in us and was already very committed to the developments in Tonga. His interest and impact on us were so significant. I still have over 60 letters Dr Vautier wrote that are interwoven with counsel, challenge and encouragement. This web of connections with people interested in the new mission to Tonga was growing.

Victor Wilson returned from Tonga at the end of 1972, and as an encouragement to be prepared, he told us of some of the conditions and the commitment that would be required, the shortages of Kiwi food and the lack of material luxuries. It was a wake-up call to the culture shock we were about to encounter.

We had one other element of God's guidance that was as painful as it was joyful. It involves an important principle anyone might be considering in long-term cross-cultural mission. Colleen's father, Ces Hilton, founder of Kiwi Ranches Rotorua and a close friend of Ernie Edwards, had taken to heart Ernie's plea from years back for workers to go to the Pacific. Ces would publicly challenge congregations to consider mission to the Pacific Islands. "Why go halfway round the world" he would ask, "when our neighbours don't know about a saving relationship with Jesus Christ?"

Then one day, he too was challenged to answer his own plea, and in response said, "Lord, even if you want one of my own children." Little did he know how deeply he would feel that challenge. So came the day Colleen told her father of our call to go to Tonga. He was quite overwhelmed but grateful. Jesus did say:

> "If anyone comes to me and does not hate his own father and mother and wife and children and brothers and sisters, yes, and even his own life, he cannot be my disciple." (Luke 14:26 NET)

Having said that, both Colleen's and my family were in full support of this pretty challenging decision for our small family to relocate indefinitely to Tonga for the sake of the gospel.
On my final visit to say goodbye to my grandfather, Mr Albert White, he said, "Graeme, I've got something for you."

He handed me NZ$500 and then said, "But it's not for you. It's for Colleen. She will need a washing machine and a fridge, so this money is for her."

It turned out that there was no electricity at the newly-built chapel, but fortunately we were able to purchase a kerosene fridge. Grandad's washing machine requirement had to wait. Our only option was a galvanised iron tub and a wooden washing board, the same as everyone else! Not a problem once the arm and back muscles had warmed up! Tongans would mock me when they came and found me bent over the washing tub! A common joke – the wife is obviously in charge of this home.

So, it was a painful parting leaving our parents, but they both were in 100 percent support of our decision.

Feet on the Ground in the Friendly Islands

On Tuesday, January 8th, 1974, with the call of God confirmed in our hearts and both excitement and trepidation, we arrived at Fua'amotu Airport, Tonga, on board an Air Pacific BAC 1.11 jet. We had a two-night lay-over in Suva, Fiji, since there was no direct flight to Tonga. A blessing in disguise because we got to spend the weekend with Uncle Foster and Aunty Gwen, who had originally suggested we pray for the Tongan students studying at their Bible School. Six months after writing to Foster for prayer items, we were answering our own prayer. God works like that sometimes.

Setting foot in Tonga, climbing down the back stairs of the plane between the tail-mounted jet engines with one-year-old Joel is still etched in our memories. We immediately boarded a rickety mini-bus and transferred to a small immigration building for entry visas. First shock, the heat! Second shock, we were only issued a three-week visa! Then followed the 30-minute journey along a potholed, dusty road with the builder of the newly-finished chapel. Bernie took us directly to the Police Headquarters since, in his mind, a three-week visa needed immediate reconsideration.

We presented our passports to the police officials, but they were returned promptly with the terse response, "Three weeks is your maximum stay, sir!"

When Bernie heard this, he was brokenhearted. "I've prayed and worked for a whole year just for you to stay three weeks. What will become of this fledgling group?" he sobbed.

I responded surprisingly, in faith, "God doesn't make mistakes. He has called us, and He will make a way."

Bernie Tolmie had been in Tonga that whole year working under extremely trying circumstances, but he'd done an amazing job with the support of enthusiastic labourers from the local congregation, as well as the bravado of the unstoppable Dr Vic Wilson. Somehow, he had a knack of getting what he wanted from suppliers, even if there were shortages. The team had poured the footings, laid a concrete floor of 25 by 15 metres, poured the bond beams and laid a few thousand blocks, all with the help of a hand concrete mixer and one wheelbarrow. That's what you did back in the day! Bernie remained in Tonga for just another two weeks and then boarded a tourist ship bound for New Zealand.

Colleen and I saw him aboard the boat as he left us, alone. It was a long quiet walk, pushing Joel back up the dusty bypass road from Queen Salote Wharf to the Halaleva Church property. We were now alone, with no palangis in our world or with us in the mission. A strange feeling.

Remember the three-week visitors visa? Well, Setaleki took the initiative and submitted a letter signed by himself and Siaosi to the Immigration Department on 29th January asking for an extension (see Appendix 3). As the letter was submitted with our passports to the Immigration Department, we felt we could get on with our new life and wait for their response. A far greater challenge was our own acclimatisation and settling into an entirely new culture.

Chapter 4

Early Challenges

Problems in the Post Office

January is nearly the hottest month in Tonga, and it was 30 plus degrees when we landed, with humidity in the 80s, ideal conditions for the breeding of unrelenting mosquitoes. Within weeks of our arrival, we were all suffering from infected mosquito bites. We had a lot to learn about the importance of protection, both day and night. Apparently, mosquitoes can sense the new blood, so they were attracted to us. Sadly, Joel was worst affected, so much so that his bites required antibiotics, of which there were none. We made our first SOS to Colleen's mother.

After a rather lengthy and quite desperate wait, we received a ticket notification in our mailbox we had a parcel. It arrived late Friday afternoon and fortunately the Post Office was open on Saturday, but only for the tourist boat that had berthed. I thought I'd ask at the counter for the parcel anyway.

"No! Not today," the girl said.

I politely asked again, explaining we were waiting for urgent medicine. The Postmaster, who was behind the wall, heard me pleading, but he was not happy. He came around and gave me a blasting in broken English.

"We don't deliver parcels on a Saturday," he shouted.

I was quite shocked, and it was hardly the way a new missionary wanted to start communicating with local officials. Feeling remorseful, I decided to try and make amends. I quickly went up the street to Talamahu Market and found a lovely ripe watermelon. I went back into the Post Office, put it on the counter and asked the girl to please give this to the Postmaster with my apologies. As I turned to leave, he came out from behind a divider to the sorting room, calling,

"Palangi, what was it you wanted?"

"Sorry, sir," I said. "We were waiting for some urgent antibiotics for our sick baby, but it's ok, I'll come in on Monday."

"Oh, no problem, just a minute," he said.

He trotted behind the dividing wall into the mail sorting area and returned with a package marked with red stickers: URGENT MEDICINE. Whew, what a relief for me, but especially for Joel. Consequently, my relationship with the Postmaster developed. Longolongo and I began a warm friendship for the duration of life in our new home. I coined a proverb for Tonga, "A sweet melon turns away wrath."

A New Home

Accommodation, too, was an immediate challenge. With Bernie being our only contact in Tonga and no reliable telephone link, arranging accommodation before we arrived wasn't an option. Therefore, finding accommodation suitable for a six-month-old proved to be difficult. From the airport, we were taken to a small bedroom provided by a Canadian volunteer who was living in a small house in the old Vaiola Motu'a (government hospital) buildings. She was supporting the project in Halaleva. After just three nights there, the church members were keen for us to move into the church accommodation. Some extra rooms had been built at the back of the main worship centre. A small two-by-three metre room with two cupboards suitable for a kitchen. Next door was a slightly larger office-type room as well as a larger youth room that got called "the ping pong room". Lastly, there was a stairway leading to a large upstairs area. It was spacious, but directly under the galvanised roof was only builders' paper, no ceiling. Temperatures were almost always 30 degrees plus, so with hot air rising and heat coming down from the iron roof, it was the proverbial "hot house". Not the best for sleeping. As mentioned earlier, there was no electricity or piped water, but a large tank collected rainwater from the roof. Lighting? We could use a small kerosene wick burner or the super lighting – a benzine light which was pumped and lit from a mantle, very bright but also giving off considerable heat, as if we needed heating!

These conditions were challenging for us with a young child, but it was great being on the church site and easily accessible for the families of the new congregation. However, there was a problem. Unbeknownst to us, the chapel building was designated for "religious purposes only". Residential living did not qualify. So, one morning we had an unexpected early visit from an inspector from the Land and Survey Department. He informed us that living in the building was illegal. We were given one week to vacate! That was a shock.

Thankfully, Setaleki and the members offered to build us a small Tongan *fale* immediately behind the chapel, this time on the land designated "residential". We quickly purchased the timber for the frame and the flooring for half of the small structure – four by three metres. The youth cut down coconut branches from the trees on site, and the ladies wove them together to make a thatched roof; the first church working bee.

Hey presto! In a week we had our new home. One half of the house had a wooden floor, the bedroom; the other half was sand

and Tongan mats; the living room. It was comfortable and convenient being next to the toilet, shower and kitchen facilities that were part of the property registered for prayer and worship.

All was quite liveable until one day, while sitting in the lounge, we spotted a large *molokau* (centipede)[13] scurrying across the mats, seemingly headed straight for Joel. He thought, "Here's something cool to play with." *Not!* Colleen freaked out and just as well. We were told later that bites can be lethal to babies. Colleen quite quickly decided this was a bit too hard to bear. So, within a month, we had reluctantly moved out of the Tongan *fale* and into a concrete block house with bedrooms, lounge, kitchen and toilet under one roof; a rental property about one kilometre away from the church building. It was a house owned by Lipoi Tupou, a local businessman.

With the initial accommodation challenges sorted and basic day-to-day living underway, it was time to settle into some of the much more significant challenges of reshaping our European styles and values.

Chapter 5

The Meeting of the Waters

When two oceans meet, having been separated by two land masses, there will be significant turbulence as the currents merge.

Colleen and I were from a New Zealand European community which valued individualism. We had a measure of independence from the wider family and a mindset that if you want something to happen it won't, unless you make it happen.

My father asked me prior to leaving, "If you are going to Tonga to plant a church, how long do you expect to be away?"

Without a thought I said, "If a guy can't plant a church in two or three years, there's something wrong with him!"

That's the response of self-confident individualism, full of arrogance, inexperience and pride. The currents of Tongan culture and currents of our European culture were about to meet with considerable turbulence. This would show particularly in the community life of the church we were called to care for and nurture into maturity.

Tonga was and is ruled by a King who exerts a strong sense of authority over the whole of society. It is far from the individualism of a democracy. On top of that, families were tightly bound together, their strength being in an extended identity, a belongingness to the village chief who was, in turn, under the authority of the village noble, the representative of the ruling monarch.

Further to the convergence of cultures, there was a significant clash around the two views of time. Watches and timetables took on a much lower priority than what we were used to.

My first initiation to this new system was simply putting petrol in the tank of the little Suzuki 90, Dad's old farm bike he sent over to help the three of us get around. I called into Burns Philip for some gas. After waiting at the pump for about 15 minutes, I walked through to the workshop to find an attendant. There they all were, resting under the shade of a rather large mango tree. Where else at 2.30 p.m. on a steamy hot afternoon! Eventually I got the petrol but started learning a core lesson – never be in a hurry!

Then came the timing of our church services. Oh dear, lots to learn. In the Western world, church services start and finish mostly at a specific time, right? Well, not necessarily so in this new world. Having said that, most people who visit Tonga are rudely woken by church bells two or three days a week around 5 a.m. And then on Sundays, when most Tongans attend services, there is a routine of bellringing that begins 15 minutes before the service starts. But the final ringing lasts about one minute, and when the final bell tolls, the first hymn begins. Sounds like a contradiction, but some of the more established churches were a lot more particular about starting on time than ours.

After about one year, Dr Wilson sent up a small Datsun with a flat deck. That's when we began collecting people from a three to four-mile radius. Until then the members would walk to church, so the starting time was when they all arrived.

One Sunday morning on our rounds to collect people, we arrived at a settlement just as the dad was heading into the outside washroom. Obviously, he had to wait while the six kids were showered first. We waited another 20 minutes until he came, finally, like, "What's the hurry?"

There was considerable lively discussion between Colleen and I for the duration of our years in Tonga about getting the church services started "on time". My view was the worship and Bible teaching is *for the people*, so what's the point in starting before the people arrive! As the years ticked by and as young leaders began to assume responsibility, they had many discussions in the leadership about how to train the congregation to respect service times. The older generation measured time by where the sun was in the sky for daily routines and what stage the moon was for fishing and agricultural purposes. Surely Solomon had profound wisdom when he wrote that time was not measured by hours and seconds but rather by periods that accompany the varied seasons of life.

> There is a time for everything,
> and a season for every activity under the heavens:
> a time to be born and a time to die,
> a time to plant and a time to uproot,
> a time to kill and a time to heal… (Ecclesiastes 3:1-3 NIV)

Solomon's time wasn't measured in seconds and hours but rather seasons and natural cycles. That is the opportune time. It took us a long time to get that!

What's Mine, What's Yours?

Possessions were always going to be a challenge to us. Personal property is far more defined in an individualistic Western culture than in a community-based culture such as the one we adopted as our place to serve Jesus. All believers are told to "look not only on your own interests, but also to the interests of others" (Philippians 2:4). Interests would involve possessions, surely. And then Jesus himself taught, "Give to everyone who asks and if anyone takes what belongs to you, do not demand it back."

In the early days, requests for many of our possessions came thick and fast. Money to buy a fishing net – now, because the moon is right for good fishing at present.

Money to get married – "When do you need it, 'cos we need to pray about it."

"Well, I want to leave tomorrow to another island and marry her!"

For the building of the chapel, one piece of equipment was absolutely necessary – a wheelbarrow! Well, it was obvious to the small church community how multi-purpose it was. Collecting *niu motu'u* (mature coconuts) that had fallen would be much easier with a wheelbarrow. There was still a lot of work to be done at the chapel, digging a septic tank, cleaning up left-over broken bricks… but where was the barrow? I visited many homes of people from the chapel trying to relocate the wheelbarrow. After all, wasn't I responsible for it? Wasn't it actually "mine"? Didn't I have rights to it? Nope, not here. New country, new set of values – I had some hard lessons to learn.

And then there was the 20,000-litre water tank to collect fresh water from the large chapel roof. Fresh water was a precious commodity in Tonga. Reticulated water was not only hard to come by – the system of piped water was very limited in the Nuku'alofa town centre and certainly not available to Halaleva on the outskirts. It was also hard water in that it had a very high calcium content – groundwater came up through the coral substrate of the islands. Also, the wells were sometimes barely above sea level. Quite unsuitable for drinking and not good for washing either.

A water tank with fresh water was a great asset to the church *and* the community. Our little home, mere metres from the tank, was a blessing, but the water needed careful management since there were long periods of no rain. The new property was now fenced, and everything inside belonged, we thought, to the church community.

Before the purchase of the land and building of the chapel, the land had been a thoroughfare of the growing settlement of Pili through to the main bypass road and bus service. So, a freshwater tank right there on the track was very convenient and was constantly visited by all and sundry. Drinking water, washing water, water for kava clubs. The large tank was barely enough for us and the church, let alone the surrounding community. And it ran out far too quickly. "So, who's water was it?" I asked. There was no answer.

I decided, therefore, to put a padlock on the tank and stop this indiscriminate use of "our" water. That surely would solve the problem, I thought, until we came home from town one day to find the plastic pipe to the tap shattered and a flood of water all around the concrete pad outside our kitchen. Someone had decided if they couldn't drink the water, then no one would. We had to learn the lesson of sharing in a way appropriate in this culture. A Tongan pastor who lived in similar circumstances where people had to ask permission to get supplies used to answer them in a unique way. "Ask the tank, not me," he'd say.

We had another challenging experience while coming to grips with cultural differences. This was a domestic issue within our new family that took us into unchartered territory. I needed to visit one family just down the road to talk about a family member who had got into difficulties outside of Tonga. So, I strolled down to the family *fale* and sat down on the floor to discuss the pretty sensitive issue of bringing the family member back home.

As the mother and I talked, I noticed her becoming increasingly agitated. She began to slowly, but deliberately, tease out her long, frizzy hair in such a way she began to look quite frightening. The longer I went on explaining, the scarier she looked – hair standing out almost witch-like. Of course, I'm speaking in English, but she is "hearing" through a Tongan cultural view of which I had virtually no appreciation. Then, without any warning, she reached for the *taufale* (general-purpose broom). It had a long handle with coconut leaf ribs tied tightly to it. The *taufale* was commonly used for keeping things neat and tidy around the home, even tidying up unruly children. But this time, she raised it above her head and slammed it onto the floor with a wallop, barely inches from my legs. She glared at me and said, "You palangi are to blame for this."

I was quite terrified and wasn't going to just sit there. Fight or flight? Like a true Kiwi ninja, I scarpered out the door, heading for home, about 400 metres away. I glanced over my shoulder at one stage, and she was coming after me with the broom above her head.

I sprinted back to Colleen and said, "Quick, she's coming!"

"Who's coming? What's happening?" said Colleen.

I quickly filled her in on the conversation.

"What should we do?" Colleen said.

"Into the small room to pray," we agreed. Without bothering to shut the door, we dropped to our knees and began to blurt out our stammering requests to the Lord for safety and wisdom. Within a couple of minutes, we heard heavy breathing at the door, but the angry lady didn't enter the room, maybe out of respect for our praying. It was a looooong prayer! Just long enough for the distressed mother's anger to abate. Colleen then stood up, went to her and put her arms around her.

"Calm down. The Lord will work this out," she said. Well, she did calm down, but not without reminding us of her desire for some sort of revenge. In hindsight, this was more of a spiritual confrontation than cultural tension, but very sobering all the same.

Learning Appreciation for Seniority

One of the more difficult barriers for people as young as Colleen and I was to develop operating principles in the confines of a small church community. Jesus lived as a Jew amongst Jews and selected young Jewish men whom he trained, all in the environment of Jewish life. In the small Christian community to which we were called, there was a group of men with quite a different understanding of the leadership principles taught by Jesus. Rather, their practices were shaped much more by Tongan culture. It took a long time for us to understand and appreciate these differences and the challenges they would present as the young church grew.

On one occasion early in our journey, I pillioned Setaleki on my Suzuki 90 down to Siaosi's seaside village, Pātangata. Siaosi and Setaleki, along with Fine, were the leaders of this new church-plant. Setaleki, in his broken English, explained that my most urgent role was to set up connections with our New Zealand churches and provide work schemes for the younger generation. This was being practised by other churches. Groups of young men and women would travel to New Zealand on work visas and send finances back to improve the home living conditions as well as pay for education.

My response to this proposal was spontaneous and direct, with no consideration or respect for their seniority. I bluntly said this would not happen.

Setaleki asked why not.

Again, I responded curtly and categorically, "Because God has called us to Tonga to preach the gospel and make disciples, as in Matthew 28."

Setaleki's retort was, "We've had the *lotu* (faith) in Tonga for over 100 years. We don't need to repeat what's already been done. If you can't set up work schemes for our youth, then you should go back to your homeland."

"I can't do that either," was my reply, "because God had called us to this mission, and we can only go back if He leads us back."

Impasse! Clash of culture. A young man not respecting seniority. A clash of spiritual understanding regarding the core nature of an evangelical church.

That was the first eye-opener for us. It seemed the senior leaders of the fellowship had a serious disconnect with the whole purpose of planting the church. In those early days, the understanding between the recognised leaders and ourselves developed into some serious and unsettling confrontations. Not knowing the language didn't help either.

As the church meetings began to take form I preferred to use the younger students from Bible School to preach sermons rather than these older men. At one point, out of sheer frustration, Siaosi said, "I'm tired of being kicked around like a *foʻi pulu* (ball), attending services but with very little involvement in them."

An obvious lack of experience on our part made these early days very difficult. I learned early on that these men had a very shallow understanding of the evangelical faith. Foster Crane, who mentored us during these years, explained that the transition from traditional church practices to a Bible-centred function would be problematic. It could take several years before leaders were reborn by His Spirit. This proved to be true.

So, meeting the cultural challenge and coming to a realisation of significant social differences had begun. Of course, even for us, it would take years to wean our hearts away from the old familiar system of church practises until we learned principles Jesus and the Apostles taught in the New Testament. But that's to be totally expected when we committed to total immersion into the culture.

After about 18 months in this challenging new world, we were feeling particularly jaded. Out of the blue, we received a letter of encouragement from New Zealand, praying for the work in Samoa. I said jokingly, "Oh, that's the problem – we're not meant to be in Tonga but Samoa!" New to us was the twenty four seven expectation of a missionary!

We did take a couple of weeks off in August 1975 in Samoa. Close friends Betty and Lloyd Brewerton provided exactly what we needed – a break away from the relentless challenges of the growing fellowship and some observing the growth of the Gospel Fellowship in Samoa, which was very refreshing.

Caring for Families

Another illustration of cultural differences occurred while visiting families of the congregation. Visiting the homes and families of our congregation was a very new experience for both parties. We were very young, with a small child, and we weren't used to sitting cross-legged on the floor for any more than a few minutes. The homes were extremely basic but very tidy. So, when the Afuhaʻamango family asked us around for the evening family devotions, that was a gesture of love and a good opportunity to share in deeper family life. Interestingly, the night we chose to travel from Kāpetā to their small home in Pili, I was feeling very nauseous. So much so we stopped the van on the roadside for me to vomit. We eventually entered their simple lounge and sat cross-legged on the floor – Colleen's mother, Mavis, Colleen, Joel and me.

Tuʻulaki announced that she would conduct the family devotions, which was quite unusual but an early indication of her strong influence in their home. She placed the Bible in her hands and proceeded to let it fall open to whatever page. She then put her finger on a verse but before reading it said, "This verse is for you, Colleen."

Tuʻulaki explained that there was judgment due to Colleen for some failures. Then a repeat of the process, but this time the verse was for Colleen's mother, Mavis. The message was not quite so severe as Colleen's verse. Then the process again, this time for me. It so happened that this verse was from the New Testament, and it contained blessing and encouragement. I'd become increasingly disturbed at the process of reading and interpreting scripture, so much so that the stomach upset had completely (miraculously?) gone!

With a certain degree of courage mixed with anger, I said, "Stop, Tuʻulaki! This is not the way to read or use scripture."

I proceeded to give an impromptu explanation of how to read the message of each text, in its context and asking questions about what the writer was trying to teach, what we could learn about God, about ourselves. I was directly contradicting this sincere lady and in her own home. To this day, I'm not sure how she handled the correction. However, it was a wake-up call to us regarding the need to teach carefully how to read and understand the Word of God.

Tuʻulaki obviously had a passion to conduct Bible Readings for her family but was ignorant of how God could speak coherently from such revelation. 2 Timothy 3:15b-17 was a great starting point:

> ...the sacred writings, which are able to make you wise for salvation through faith in Christ Jesus. All Scripture is breathed out by God and profitable for teaching, for reproof, for correction, and for training in righteousness, that the man of God may be complete, equipped for every good work.

> Do your best to present yourself to God, a worker who has no need to be ashamed, rightly handling the word of truth. (2 Timothy 2:15)

New Food Experiences

Nothing is more immediate, even confrontational, than our cultural preferences of diet. No meat and three vegetables the way we were bought up in New Zealand. Tonga has some of the richest volcanic soils in the Pacific, so there is no lack of potential for growing great vegetables.

The large food and handicraft market, Talamahu, in the centre of Nukuʻalofa, was an unforgettable first-time experience. There were yams, sometimes over a metre tall, and varieties of bananas never seen before: Misa Peka (Mr Baker's), a short fat and sweet banana;[14] hopa and pata, a green varieties best made into a desert or fried or baked in an *umu* (underground oven); and then the traditional one, bigger and sweeter than anything from a New Zealand supermarket. Varieties of fruit never seen before by a couple of Kiwis, and flavours that needed definitely to be acquired.

Much of the experience of our food-tasting was provided generously at our Sunday lunches. Each Sunday, after our morning service, Tuʻulaki and Setaleki would bring a Sunday meal to us. The first time we opened the lovely, covered tray, there was a bundle of cooked hot banana leaves. Unpacking it gave us quite a surprise. Inside was something not dissimilar in appearance to what cows leave behind in the paddock. Right, a cow pat.

"What in the world is that!" Colleen exclaimed.

Well, we were up for anything new, so in we went. Cooked taro leaves wrapped around tinned beef, diced onion, sauced with thick coconut cream, called a *lū pulu*. Wow, the flavour was indescribably delicious.

Later in the day, Tuʻulaki asked if the *lū* was *ngako*. Quickly referring to our dictionary, we saw *ngako* meant "fatty".

"Oh no," we said, "very nice." Well saying no to that question was both an insult and a contradiction. *Ngako* also means "rich" – as in creamy – and saying no meant the *lū* was poor quality! But to say it was nice to Tuʻulaki also didn't make sense. Both we and our new Tongan family were on a steep learning curve in communication and cuisine.

I got to love *lū* so much and ate so much each Sunday that it took at least a day to get over stomach cramps and other internal murmurings. It took probably six months before our palates and digestive programming were reset, and then Pacific Island food and different cooking methods became our new way of living. There were always shortages of what we would have eaten back home, like roast lamb and gravy, but taro, yam, papaya, octopus and kumara were now becoming the delicious new norm.

Chapter 6

Learning Language and Culture

Probably the most acute challenge in this story of the clash of cultures, at least for us, was that relating to language. As first-time language learners, we were immediately confronted with the necessity of authentic communication, especially since the goal was to connect on a spiritual level. That was an absolute necessity to growing Christian community in the church.

Culturally, Tongans showed great respect and deference toward palangis, since it was missionaries from Britain who originally settled and formally established Christian churches. However, it was Tongans themselves who were responsible for the spreading of the Good News of Jesus Christ throughout their islands.

For a small congregation like ours, previously unexposed to palangis, taking leadership from a couple as young as Colleen and I would be a challenge, so learning the language was critical. Unbeknownst to us, we were about to experience what is called "immersion". Isn't that a reflection of what "incarnation" means? Having one's mind, values, even emotions reshaped by learning a language and adapting deeply to the culture one is seeking to reach?

The unforgettable Ernie Edwards introduced this to us back in the Bible School days in Kaitoke. How would we begin to learn the Tongan language? It never crossed our minds; we had just crossed the ocean and were about to find out.

In the providence of God, within the first month of arriving, the Lord arranged a meeting with Nigel and Melenaite Statham. This was destined to be a significant building block for the mission as well as provide both of us with a valuable camaraderie for over a decade.

Nigel, an Australian teacher, linguist-come-archaeologist, nicknamed "Digger", was married to a finely cultured young teacher, Melenaite, from Lakepa Village on Tongatapu Island, who was born, raised and educated in Tonga. They were young, deeply committed Christians and members of the Free Wesleyan Church. They remain to this day among the most precious gifts God provided for our mission.

Based on an offer from Nigel, we formally began the discipline of language learning. We would walk the two dusty kilometres down the potholed road from Halaleva to Vaolōloa to the Statham's humble dwelling. Nigel introduced us to a very helpful resource, Dr Eric Shumway's Intensive Course in Tongan – 136 lessons of vocabulary and grammar with basic practice sentences for each lesson. But the prophetic words Nigel gave in one of our first lessons were what made the difference.

"If you want to reach Tongan people with the gospel," he said, "you will accomplish more in one year with the language than you could in ten years without it."

That was all the motivation we needed. We'd come to preach Christ in the most efficient way possible. But as well as the weekly rigour of the lessons, Nigel was a tyrant for correct pronunciation, giving us a diction that was eventually to so impress the local community that we were asked many times if we actually had a Tongan upbringing! That's quality teaching as well as spiritual enabling.

What also helped was that we are both natural musicians with a keen ear for sound. Providence at work again, don't you think? It took us at least two years before we began to break through the "shame" barrier of speaking Tongan as much and as often as we could. But one other breakthrough moment in the arduous journey came by way of a deep spiritual conviction relating to our spontaneous participation in church services.

In the Gospel Church tradition, men were given an open opportunity to share in weekly service, to share thoughts, read hymns or pray during the celebration of the Lord's Supper. Men were expected to contribute to the praise of Jesus Christ. As I began to understand more of what men were saying, I grew increasingly frustrated at not being able to participate. I used to contribute briefly in English, but could see from the blank looks that nothing of what I said was understood. At the end of one Sunday morning service, I was despondent at this barrier. I was so convicted that during the service, I quietly prayed, "Lord, I desperately want to be able to worship in the local language so our hearts are knit with the congregation. Today I commit not to speak again in the church in English. If I can't say it in Tongan, I won't speak at all."

I didn't receive a miraculous gift of the language, but instead a serious determination to prepare well by practising reading from the Tongan Hymnbook or reading something from one of the two Bibe translations.

The next Sunday, I simply read a Tongan hymn and understood all the truth it was offering about Jesus Christ. What a thrill when Fepaki, one of the older ladies who couldn't speak a word of English, came and said, "*Mālō 'aupito Kulemi. Sai aupito ho'o lea fakatonga.*" (Thank you, your Tongan speaking was great.)

The service format provided several weekly opportunities; to practise reading Scripture and hymns in a public environment, to listen carefully and understand what others said so my contribution would be connected to theirs, to hear what was precious to new believers and the overflowing of hearts in praise for the gospel. That's not to say I wasn't nervous and usually sweated profusely while speaking, but it was all part of reprogramming our hearts as we heard what moved them about God's love for them through Christ.

Another great help in the language learning process was the impromptu visits of T. Maile, an ageing and very likeable man. He'd visit our little kitchen quite regularly on his way home from work. He appeared tired and hungry, so we shared what we had in our pot. Exactly what you did in Tonga if you arrived during mealtime.

T would suddenly walk into our kitchen.

"*Ha'u 'o kai, T,*" (Come and eat, T) was the perfect thing to say.

Having a tutor like him was perfect for us in many ways. He was as authentic a speaker as you'd find anywhere; he couldn't understand hardly a word of English. And his services came without charge. Colleen would offer him cold water from the fridge.

"*Mālō 'aupito,*" (Thanks very much) he'd say, and then start talking loud and long. No, not one word of English, as I said, he knew none.

On this memorable day, he was there in semi-darkness, sitting on the small concrete step leading into our tiny kitchen. Suddenly, out of the darkness appeared these brown millipedes, scores of them. We could have trodden on them and heard the crunch, but would have to clean up the mess.

"*Omai ha hina,*" he said.

We learned from Nigel, our language tutor, that *omai* meant "bring me". But *hina*? What did he mean? The dictionary had about four options. The first was pumpkin! Why would he want a pumpkin? But we got him one.

"*Ikai, 'ikai,*" he said, with a great laugh. "*Palangi vale*" (Stupid palangis).

"*Omai ha hina,*" he insisted.

We looked again. *Hina* = spider. This guy is whacked, we thought! Lesson: the native speaker is *never* wrong! No, he didn't want a spider. Another look, *hina* can also mean "white" as in white-haired. Or a glass or jar. Hey presto, we got a jar, and immediately he laughed and began to fill the jar with millipedes. Learned that lesson – the same word has many meanings.

But many lessons were done late in the evening beside a hot kerosene light and in 30-plus degree heat. One night I slammed the book shut in frustration. Colleen was getting along well.

"Too hard," I muttered. "I'll never do it," and went up the stairs to bed.

When relating this to Nigel, he reminded us that language learning can be compared to climbing a mountain; long grinding ridges of sweat with no summit in sight, then a plateau to catch your breath and a view of the peak, only to find another ridge even steeper. It's a long, slow slog, but the view from the top will be a great reward. To be able to teach and preach God's Word in the native tongue was "the view" we knew would make all the effort worthwhile.

Haafe Houa mo e Kōsipeli (The Gospel Half Hour)

After two years of language tuition, Nigel said, "I've done about as much tuition as you need. The rest is up to you."

It was just then Colleen came up with this crazy idea, "Why don't we do a Radio programme?

You see, she remembered how her father had started Kiwi Gospel Hour and broadcast the gospel over HCJB Ecuador for several of her growing years. She sensed the impact radio evangelism could have in our mission.

I was quite petrified. I'll never forget the day, after praying together perhaps for a week or two, going down to the A3Z radio station office on the little Suzuki 90 and enquiring of the then station manager, Tavake Fusimālohi.

A3Z was founded in 1961 by Queen Salote, Tupou III, and operates as a service of the Tonga Broadcasting Commission (TBC). Its slogan is "The Call of the Friendly Islands". I was hesitant to ask the manager, since we were a new church presenting ourselves to a country with already strongly established denominations, to say nothing of preaching in Tongan! To be honest, I secretly hoped he would ask me to bring a sample. Instead, Tavake said, "You can start a monthly programme next week."

No pressure. I went home trembling and told Colleen. She just said, "Halleluia! Prayer answered."

I hurried off to my missionary friend and consultant, Nigel. As usual, he made us an amazing offer of his expertise. If I would write the sermon in English, he would translate it into Tongan. I'd type it up, practise reading it, and then read it back to him. He would correct my pronunciation and was ruthless about me sounding as authentic as possible. We stood in front of a mirror with a paper in front of our lips, pronouncing p's and t's without the paper moving – technically, as an aspirant sound rather than an expletive – enough of that.

Once the sermon was practised and ready, the moment of truth – go down to the recording studio. When the red light came on, it was time to shine. For the first few month's programmes, we went with a small team of singers and used the Hammond organ in the studio and my guitar as accompaniment, singing one or two songs as an introduction.

Fifty years later, *Haafe Houa mo e Kōsipeli* (The Gospel Half Hour) is still being broadcast with similar consistent positive feedback from the community – "Your teaching of the Bible is non-political, nondenominational, but clearly gospel-centred." Praise be to God!

We learned so many new aspects of the Tongan language because of starting the Radio broadcast. Just weeks before we finally returned to New Zealand, I had an impromptu meeting with a Tongan advisor to senior English teachers from the Education Department. She wanted to know the process of our language learning that had made us so proficient. She wanted to duplicate those principles in the opposite direction, Tongan students learning to speak English. I went through the various processes; weekly lessons, concentration on diction, reading out loud, speaking wherever and whenever I could.

"No," she said, "I teach all this. There's got to be something else."

My response was, "Jesus Christ commissioned us to come to Tonga to preach the gospel. Because he laid down his life, we did the same in language learning. It must be His Spirit helping us."

"That's it," she said, "It's like a gift from God, and I can't teach that."

Language and Grasping for the Soul of the Culture

The discipline of language learning extended far beyond the ability to communicate verbally. It was the doorway into a whole different social structure and value system. For example, just as there are three strata in Tongan society – royalty, nobility and commoners – there are three variations of terms for each of these strata in the language. Firstly, terms and structures that apply to commoners, secondly to the nobility and thirdly to royalty. To be able to use these terms appropriately is a significant mark of respect for authority around which Tongan society is built.

A variety of common greetings were a significant acknowledgement of an individual's belonging in society and their status or position of authority. For example, functional greetings are made based around the work or activity people may be doing when you meet them. *"Mālō e ngāue"* (Thank you for working). For those doing general manual tasks: *"mālō e tafi"* (thank you for sweeping) – to ladies cleaning their yards, a common chore keeping one's yard tidy. Even *"mālō e mo'ui"* (thank you for being alive) – to those you haven't met for a while; or *"mālō 'etau mo e faingata'a"* (thank you that we can share in your grief) – to those who are mourning at a funeral. The general greeting, *"Mālō e lelei"* is an acknowledgement of being well.

Knowing and using the variety of such greetings is a beautiful expression of community and solidarity with others. It provides an immediate connection even with the life of a stranger. When it comes from someone obviously from another culture, it provides a silent identification of those two people that can eventually lead to conversations that might be gospel-centred. It's an integral part of the incarnation principle required for cross-cultural evangelism.

I clearly remember learning for the first time how to greet someone walking towards me on the road. *"Na'á ke 'i fē?"* ("Where have you been?") is the typical greeting. A Kiwi might respond by telling the other person to mind their own business, but in Tonga it's an acknowledgement of the fact that people are moving around and getting on with life. One of the local youths took it on himself to teach me this simple yet significant aspect of Tongan culture.

Chapter 7

Medical Challenges and Painful Times

The health of our family was something that forced us to grow in our faith and face the reality of living in a new environment within a new health system. Dengue, hepatitis, headlice and scabies were all there waiting for an opportune time to take us down and come they did.

Our second child, Janita, came along in 1975. Colleen had experienced complications during Joel's birth, so she was rather nervous and wanted confidence in the gynaecologists. Dr Maka Taumoepeau and his British wife Bridget had become good friends through our children attending kindergarten together.

While Janita's birth went fine, she developed a serious cross-eyed problem before she was one year old. She was seen by the resident eye specialist Dr Taumoepeau, who assured us he could perform the delicate operation. It felt like a great challenge to our faith to entrust Janita to the local specialists. It was certainly a traumatic experience handing her over for the operation. I can still hear her screaming as we walked away down the corridor.

The operation seemed to indicate success for a year; however, a second operation was necessary, this time done in New Zealand. Through this, we endeavoured to show our trust in God and trust in the Tongan specialists.

As mentioned, two health encounters involved repeated experiences with the dreaded dengue and one with hepatitis. Late in

1979, I became very lethargic and noticed a significant yellowing on the bed sheets from perspiration. Our doctor friend, Bridget Taumoepeau, suggested I bring in a urine sample.

When she saw it, she laughed and said, "You've filled this with Coca Cola right?"

"Of course not, what's wrong?"

"Well, in that case," she said, "You've got hepatitis!"

I still remember sleeping outside under a mango tree. The fever was high, and the air temperature unbearable. It was at least a month before I started regaining some energy.

Dengue fever, on the other hand, was a much harder condition to overcome. Both Colleen and I had repeats of this horrible virus. Every year another strain seemed to sweep the country with varying symptoms. Nausea, vomiting, rashes, aches and pains, including eye pain typically behind the eyes, muscle, joint, or bone pain. The warning that many didn't heed was, "Don't go back to work too soon."

Relapses were common, and both of us suffered. Dengue fever had a more far-reaching impact on the population than COVID-19.

These experiences were part of our being immersed in the common life of the community. The church community was extremely generous, providing food and fruit during these tough times.

Early in our first year, we met up with Ewan and Gillian Laurenson from Hutt Valley, a couple who were VSA workers. Together, we began to offer basic First Aid two days a week. A very poor couple living close by, Inoke and Taufa, came seeking help with their children. They were very helpful as we practised language with them.

Colleen's dad kept up to date with our beginnings in this small First Aid venture. He decided to send some of Dr Schuessler's Cell Salts, apparently used for a wide variety of ailments. Colleen read up and found the salts had some benefits for women with conception issues. One day, a lady was sharing her problem, so Colleen gave her some of the salts to try. Well, hey presto, a month later she came back so excited. She was pregnant! That caused a stir, and many women came with similar problems but not the same result.

In the mid-70s, church ministers and other expatriate representatives were invited to join the Vaiola Hospital Board to raise funds for the great needs. On Christmas 1978, the Board decided to visit the hospital to give out simple gifts and bring good wishes to the people. While walking through the isolation ward, I noticed the birth date on one patient's bed, 24.12.1948. That was my birthdate!

I greeted the patient, Siaosi Sandys. He looked pale and emaciated, and I felt a strong sense of compassion for him. I waited behind while the rest of the board members went to the next ward and asked Siaosi if there was anything I could get him.

"Some *vai melie* (fresh water), please."

"I'm going to New Zealand tomorrow," I said, "but I'll bring you a bottle today, and when I come back, I'll come and visit."

Unbeknownst to me, he was sick with infectious Tuberculosis (TB). Long story short, when we returned, I not only got him water, but after he had been discharged, I met his estranged wife and got them back together. We started Bible studies, and after some time, he and his wife, Neta, drank the Water of Life. Both came to faith and became part of the fellowship.

Some six months later, we heard banging on our bedroom window in Kāpetā about 2 a.m. in the morning.

"*Kulemi, kulemi*, come quickly, Siaosi has died!" Neta cried out.

Sadly, he passed away with three young children. I took his funeral service and at the gravesite, explained to the very large gathering how Siaosi and I began acquaintance at the hospital. Then he became my friend. We visited one another's houses and families. Then, eventually, he became my brother by personal faith in Jesus Christ. To this day, we remain close friends of the Sandys family.

One more medical emergency is worth relating, as it taught us much about a mindset around diseases with which we were unfamiliar.

On one of our regular Bible study evenings, we arrived at Tuʻulaki's house to find her youngest daughter, Toulini, very sick. On enquiry, we found she'd been vomiting and with a fever for a few days.

As normal Tongan medicines were tried with no avail, Tuʻulaki was very concerned and asked me to pray for Toulini's healing. I was glad to do that, but asked Tuʻulaki if I could add a condition to my prayer. The condition was that if Toulini hadn't recovered significantly by morning, she should be taken to the hospital. Tuʻulaki tentatively agreed since it was commonly held that prayers of faith, particularly from pastors, could cure all sicknesses.

Morning came, and we found out Toulini had been taken urgently to hospital overnight as she had started foaming around the mouth and had a high fever. Just a few days later, we discovered Toulini had spiked herself on a nail while playing outside and that she had been diagnosed with tetanus. This drew us closer to Tuʻulaki's family while helping us understand we had a lot to learn about the community's understanding of faith and use of the medical profession.

As you can see, medical and health issues were shared with our newly developing family. Our immersion into society became transformative, very real and intensely personal. It was a significant part of collectively working out our faith in daily life.

Pain and Loss

Perhaps the experience that has taken Tonga's communal love most deeply into our hearts occurred in 1983 with the loss of our fourth child, Brent. Colleen was advised to return to New Zealand for Brent's birth because of similar complications experienced during her pregnancy with Joel.

Brent was born on 19 February 1982; however, because of swallowing difficulties, milk flooded his lungs, so he was given specialist treatment for five weeks and recovered. I had returned to New Zealand with Colleen for the birth, but after Brent had settled into early routines, I flew back to Tonga.

Cyclone Isaac had swept through the southern islands of Tongatapu and Ha'apai where there was considerable devastation, so I decided to return and help with our families who were worst affected.

On Friday 7 May, I talked on the phone with Colleen around 9 a.m. At 11.30 a.m., while completing errands in Nuku'alofa, I met a friend who told me Nigel and Melenaite had been trying to contact me urgently. I quickly rode over on the motorbike to their place. Devastating news, Colleen had laid Brent in bed after his morning feed. She returned from hanging out washing some 15 minutes later to find he was no longer breathing. He had passed away because of "obscure natural causes", known then as Cot Death (Sudden Infant Death Syndrome – SIDS).

I flew back to New Zealand that afternoon, and we laid Brent in a grave at the Waikumete Cemetery on Monday 10 May. It was precious to us that our great friend Naisa, who was studying at Auckland University, carried Brent's coffin for us. We decided after a week of mourning that we would follow the sound advice of an inspiring poem we found quoted in a book by Elizabeth Elliot:

Do the Next Thing

Do it immediately, do it with prayer,
Do it reliably, casting all care;
Do it with reverence, tracing His hand

Who placed it before thee with earnest command.
Stayed on Omnipotence, safe 'neath His wing,
Leave all resultings, do the next thing.[15]

The next thing for us was to return to Tonga, which we did. On arrival, we wondered how our congregation would react. Infant deaths were common, but we were to learn the beautiful nature of Tongan compassion. Leaving New Zealand was painful, but we landed in Tonga with a strange emptiness. There were none of our dearest friends at the airport to meet us, which we found surprising. But as we drove into our home in Ananā, the outside yard was full of all those dear friends, dressed in full mourning attire.

On entering the front door, there was a large circle of people seated on the floor with bowed heads. In the centre of the room, placed on special tapa cloth, was a small roasted pig. The leaders proceeded to lead us in some of the great hymns of hope, followed by the scriptures upon which that hope rests. The memory of that gathering placed an indelible sense of love and respect in our hearts for our spiritual family. Those He has redeemed will be the ones we spend eternity with.

Over the years, the loss of our dear Brent has given many opportunities to share the comfort of God with others who need that comfort.

Chapter 8

Starting Foundations

While this story traces our journey to Tonga and the establishment of the Tonga Gospel Churches, it is clearly obvious that the Spirit of God was at work long before we even thought of Tonga as a mission field. He was calling the hearts of the nationals, using them as his instruments to establish a foothold for such a work to begin. What follows are testimonies of just a small sample of people God used in these beginning foundations.

'Ofa Fatafehi (An Unlikely Conversion)

I grew up with my family in the Ha'apai group of islands in the early '70s, with seven other siblings. I was studying in Ha'apai and attended a Mormon middle school. I passed the exam which qualified me to further my education at the main Mormon High School, Liahona, on the main island of Tongatapu.

I was the only one of the family my parents could afford to send to school. However, there was one requirement before I could continue at Liahona; to be baptised into the Mormon Church. In preparation for this rite, I was taught nothing about Mormon teachings, just that I must be baptised. That was the devil's way of getting me into the church.

My family decided to relocate to Tongatapu both for my education and for better economic opportunities. Once in

Liahona, I quickly learned the aim of every student, indeed the best way to make quick progress was to get as many family baptised into the Mormon Church.

I succeeded in getting my mother and many of my siblings, but not Siaosi, my father. I tried so hard, but he refused, saying, "I'll die with the Gospel Church. If yours is the true Church, how come you won't respect your father and join with the Gospel Church?"

Siaosi had been asking me to go to Fiji and study at the Bible School where Foster Crane was training some of our young people. I thought, "Ok, I'll do what he says – Go to Foster's Bible School, but in reality, it'll be a holiday."

That was 1972. While there, I caused a lot of problems. I would run away at night with some of my Tongan friends. No sooner had I arrived when one of the students, Narayan Nair, asked me straight out, "'Ofa, are you a Christian?"

"Of course, don't you know, all Tongans are Christian?" I replied.

I felt insulted he even asked.

But he persisted. "No, 'Ofa, only those who are born again are Christians."

I passed it off as if he was just being judgmental, but the question never left me.

Eventually, Foster caught us running away at night and threatened to send us back. I was afraid and pleaded with Foster, saying, "If you send us back, Siaosi will kill me."

We returned at the end of 1972, just as the foundations of the Halaleva Church building were started. Foster came over to see how the building was going. My father and Setaleki decided to hold an open-air preaching service with Foster in our village, Pātangata.

Seta directed me to translate Foster's sermon. I said I

wasn't good enough. But he persisted, saying, "What's the point of going to Fiji for training if when you come back you can't do anything!"

So, with some nervousness I agreed. While I was translating Foster's sermon, our benzine light ran out of fuel, leaving us in the dark. But Victor Wilson started up his bomb of a car. On came the headlights. But I wished he had left us in the dark.

That night, Foster was preaching from Job. His subject was, "Can you count the number of your sins?"

> How many are my iniquities and sins?
> Show me my transgression and my sin. (Job 13:23 NIV)

The open field, where we used to play soccer and volleyball, was full of people who knew me and my family. I was trying to translate for the preacher, but the Spirit of God was working on my heart as I was translating his words. Foster said,

> "Though it is impossible to count your sins, they can all be forgiven by the sacrifice Jesus Christ made on the cross. You must bring your sinful life to Him, invite Christ into your life as your Saviour, and they will all be wiped off God's record."

I had never heard this teaching in my life, certainly not from the Mormon Church. I remember many people responding that night to Foster's message by committing themselves to Jesus Christ. And I, the translator, a Mormon, was feeling guilty of my own spiritual lostness.

After the meeting, we all went back up to our church property in Halaleva for supper. The building materials were stacked up around the property. We packed in and around Setaleki and Tuʻulaki's house.

While they were all talking about the evening, I scurried away into the piles of concrete blocks. I looked up at the starry night and knew God was watching. There, I confessed my sins and opened my heart to Jesus Christ. I remember just how dark it was, just like my sin-filled heart. No floor had yet been poured, just the footings, but in the midst of the blocks, I made a decision upon which I'd build the rest of my life. I wanted a personal relationship with God through Jesus Christ. I trusted Him to remove all my sins as He promised and committed my life to serving him. That night, Jesus Christ saved me. He made me a child of God according to John's Gospel:

> To all who did receive him, who believed in his name, he gave the right to become children of God. (John 1:12)

I told Foster in the morning what I'd done. He seemed quite shocked but was very happy. He insisted on my return to complete my last year of study, and so I did. That was 1973. I was baptised in Fiji at the Coral Coast Bible School.[16]

'Ofa and his wife Mary (Miller), from Fiji, were married in 1979. From very early in the story of the growth of the ministry, he showed a keen interest to be at the heart of evangelism and church leadership. 'Ofa and I engaged in numerous visits to villages on Tongatapu and across many of the islands. His companionship was invaluable, since it was accompanied by an incessant desire to help all to understand that a personal relationship with Jesus Christ was of greater significance than any other involvement or experience with church. In hindsight, I realised how critical this mindset is to the growth of an evangelical church.

Atunaisa Ngalu Hears the Good News

The district where the church was built was a popular place for new residents to find a plot of land and erect their simple dwellings. Many were migrating from the Vava'u and Ha'apai Islands, looking for a brighter future. It was also easy walking distance to the main secondary schools. Education was a primary reason for migrating to Tongatapu.

Amongst them was a family from Tungua Ha'apai, Asi and Fatai Ngalu. They had four children: Naisa, Losa, Fine and Mafi. As youth do, they banded together, walking to school and working together to help their families with the basics of living – gathering firewood, planting small gardens and feeding the family pigs.

A group of about eight teenage boys became known as the "Halaleva Gang". They would, however, get into certain types of relatively innocent mischief while roaming into the big city to dances, movies, or to hang out. Inevitably they got into skirmishes with other bands of *kau haua* (mischief-makers), particularly from different schools.

At first, no one knew the significance of building a small room at the back of the Chapel that became known as the Ping-Pong room. Bernie Tolmie, the builder, had introduced the inquisitive youth to table tennis. All that to say, this Halaleva Gang began to frequent the ping-pong room, and so naturally began to ask questions about this new church.

Naisa, the oldest son of Fatai and Asi, started attending some Sunday evening services with the rest of the gang. Naisa was attending Atenisi Institute, where he was exposed to refreshing and challenging academic studies under Professor Futa Helu. One momentous night, after he attended an evangelistic service in the Chapel, he had an encounter with the Eternal One, very similar to Sioeli Pulu. He was walking out the back of the church property when he was prompted to look up into the starry night sky.

In a moment of inspiration, he said, "God, if you are there, I want to know you."

When asked to tell his own story in a little more detail, this was his response:

> It's better for others to assess the change that God may make in a life. He chooses any mule who will carry His Good News to their family, village, even to the world. The mule is totally unaware of himself. People don't look to the mule, but the person or the goods he bears.
>
> One of the blessings of the Gospel Fellowship is that there have been many mules who have travelled near and far, bringing the truth of scripture upon their backs. That truth has taken many years to turn us from self-centredness to Christ-centredness, from work-centred religion to grace-centred faith for our salvation. That's what's made the gospel undiluted and brought maximum impact to our people. Like the common hymn says, "In Christ alone, our hope is found."[17]

Naisa's conversion had an impact on the Halaleva gang. A few weeks after that night under the stars, he was baptised at the foreshore of Pātangata. His other gang mates were not happy, so according to one of them, Inoke, they took the afternoon to *maumau Sapate* (break the Sabbath), roaming the streets and getting up to mischief, even making an umu of someone's poor straying dog! But God was at work, and over the ensuing months, nearly all the gang came to faith and became a team of evangelists and disciple-makers. A new gospel gang for the Halaleva Church. God's promises were being fulfilled before our eyes:

> If anyone is in Christ, he is a new creation. The old has passed away; behold, the new has come. (2 Corinthians 5:17)

Naisa has been, and is to this day, a formidable force promoting the gospel of God's grace and the truthfulness of scripture, along with the absolute necessity of the local church for the nurturing of new believers.

After graduating from Atenisi Institute, he spent some years studying at Auckland University (1985-87). During those years in New Zealand, he was cared for and nurtured by Mr Vine Martin of Kohimarama, Auckland. Vine played a significant part in caring for this young believer in a foreign land with all its temptations.

Naisa returned and eventually committed himself to teaching and preaching the Word in the four Gospel churches. Naisa has been the mainstay of pastoral care and has maintained faithfully the teaching of God's Word in the churches and through radio and television programmes for the past 50 years.

Inoke Feki

Another of the early conversions was one of Naisa's closest friends, Inoke Feki. This is his story:

> I was brought up in the Catholic Church but had very little interest in attending services. In 1975, I began attending activities at the Gospel Fellowship with my schoolmates. That occurred because of a long friendship I had with Paula

and Unga Afuhaʻamango, Seta and Tuʻulaki's sons. We were friends from primary school days.

When my mother heard about it, she was very angry and chased me from my home. I found myself having meals at Paula's home in Fanga. I found a connection with other youth and was part of the Halaleva Gang. We often roamed around Nukuʻalofa, going to dances and getting involved in fights.

I would sometimes listen to Pentecostal open-air preaching and heard something quite different from my Catholic teachings. I was familiar with Catholic rituals and had been accepted to receive the sacrament. Some of the gang were keen to be part of the Gospel Church activities, so I joined them in going along. Many times, to their open-air preaching.

I was invited to attend their Easter Camp in 1976, and through the preaching of Penaia Samusamauvondre from Fiji, I trusted in Jesus Christ alone to save me. I was very shy to let this be known in public. After camp, one of the leaders, Ofa, helped me to understand and be sure of my commitment to Christ. I was baptised down at the sea in Touliki. There was a small hole in the sea that was being dug out for a swimming pool.

My uncle happened to be walking past on the road and spotted me. He yelled loudly at me to come out of the water. "I'll kill you!" he screamed.

I looked at my uncle and then back at Graeme and made my decision. I wanted to follow Christ. I was sure about what I was doing.

I first shared my story in an open-air close to the cinema in Nukuʻalofa. One of my neighbours yelled out, "You're a Catholic! Come away from that new church. We are the true Church. The new churches are evil."

My mother is now 91 and still calls me to come back to my first church, but I tell her, "You can't take me to heaven with you, my faith is in Christ. He is the Way the Truth and the Life."

In 1977, I went to Vava'u and walked from Neiafu all over the Island. I just wanted to share with people the knowledge of God. When I came back, I went across to Deuba Bible School and learned a lot from Foster Crane. For me, the way of the Gospel Fellowship teaching was very different in that I learned so much from direct study of Scripture. There was a lot of friendship and real Christian community inside the church.

When I started attending the Gospel Fellowship, I was already involved in helping to build the Basilica, the largest Catholic church in Tonga. A lot was going on in my heart, but the simplicity of the church services in Halaleva was very meaningful. That attracted me. I started looking into the Scripture for myself.

In the Catholic services, only the bishop was able to teach the Bible. I became consumed with learning from the Word. Colleen and Graeme were very easy to get on with. 'Ofa and our youth were always in their house. My old friends were not interested, but I really was. I sensed something strong and true that I needed to know.

Thinking back after 46 years, I hear many of the same things, but there's always something new, something wonderful. I learned the grace of God came to me only when we studied the Scriptures. This happened between 1976 through 1982.

Then I left Tonga and went to Australia. I didn't find a church community and started to turn back to the disturbed mindset from my early years in Tonga. I got married, we had a child who I held for one hour, and then she died. I asked God why. My wife wanted a family, and soon our marriage broke.

Sadly, I went away from my faith for 16 years. I asked God to take my life because of my guilt of falling away from Him. I felt totally worthless. But he brought me through.

I married a friend from my earlier years, Lusi. We had a child whom we named Henry. When he was three, Lusi told me she was returning to the church. She begged me to come, but I was too ashamed. Then, on the Sunday of Easter 1998, I had a crisis. Lusi had been attending the Easter services, continually asking me to join her.

On that Sunday, she took Henry, and as they left the house, I was distraught. I cried and soon after I decided to go to the service on my own. I went inside and found Lusi and Henry. When the preacher explained again about the death and resurrection, all the truth flooded back into my heart. I poured out my sins again in true confession. He brought me back. I had walked away, but He was so faithful and would not let me go.

From that point on, it's been all for Him. I gave Henry to the Lord. I began to pray with deep passion for my son and family. Henry is now married to a beautiful Christian woman Shenaiah. Oh, what grace and patience God has shown to me.[18]

Chapter 9

Building a Local Church

While these conversions were a very positive starting foundation for our mission of church-planting, it is worth discussing the lack of preparation we had for the task. This will further highlight the mysterious work of God. When Paul was addressing the Corinthian church, he made comments that paralleled with our plight:

> For consider your calling, brothers: not many of you were wise according to worldly standards, not many were powerful, not many were of noble birth. But God chose what is foolish in the world to shame the wise; God chose what is weak in the world to shame the strong; God chose what is low and despised in the world, even things that are not, to bring to nothing things that are, so that no human being might boast in the presence of God. (1 Corinthians 1:26-29)

We had had very little formal instruction in the process of establishing an evangelical church, still less in establishing a new church in a society saturated with, even entrenched in Christian denominations. We knew practically nothing about the history of divisions that had, over a 50-year period in the early 1800s, fragmented the original Wesleyan Mission in Tonga.

In his thesis (2007), Heneli Niumeitolu makes some telling observations about this fragmentation and the reasons why the gospel of the New Testament did not take deep root:

From the start the chiefs were not only interested in the Wesleyan Mission for religious but also for political reasons; indeed, they made and even still make no such separation. Because of this collusion of the Free Wesleyan Church (FWC) and the state, the FWC is recognised as the supporter of the status quo, its ministers being part of the elite system of social and spiritual control. The ensuing confusion between the church, Christ, and culture leads to a neglect of the poor and marginal and a failure to speak prophetically to the elite.[19]

We weren't entirely without a core understanding, from our reading of the New Testament, that local churches were built, most significantly, out of various forms of culturally-sensitive evangelism centred on a local community of born-again believers. This was the special part of our upbringing through the Gospel Churches of New Zealand. We both had, since birth, been part of small but vibrant local churches – I in Te Kuiti and Nelson, and Colleen in Tokoroa, Putaruru, Paeroa and Rotorua.

In her late teens, Colleen played a significant part in the leadership of small groups of youth who attended the very popular Kiwi Ranches. She'd helped many to begin a journey of personal faith and trust in Christ but didn't have a lot of experience in connecting these new converts with youth groups within the community of a local church. A couple of years at Bible School in Auckland gave her a very basic but valuable overview of the Bible. What Colleen did have in great measure was a deep passion to share Christ with anyone who came within her sphere of life; something she had seen modelled so powerfully by her mum and dad within their home and the local church.

Arriving in Tonga with a very young child attracted the young women to her, by which we were able to establish close relationships involving deep trust. It was her passion and love for people that quickly endeared her to the small group of youth in this new church.

Formal training in mission for Colleen may have been thin, but the evangelism and discipleship of her upbringing made up for any other lack.

I, on the other hand, while benefiting greatly in my childhood years in the Te Kuiti church, experienced a personal revival in my late teens.

Upon arriving in Nelson in 1969, I was freshly impacted by the Holy Spirit with a deep desire to make Christ known in any and every community I was found to be. The Bible came alive when I stumbled upon the Navigators Bible Memory programme. Nothing is like the Word of God to breathe new life into a sleepy soul.

In my initial enthusiasm to witness, I'd take lunch hours to visit the Nelson Church steps or parks near my workplace in the hope of creating conversations about Christ. One day, while sitting with a stranger on a bench in the Queen's Gardens. I was prompted to initiate a conversation. Having no idea about how to start and seeing ducks swimming by in the stream, I took the plunge (no pun intended) and said, "Sir, have you any idea where those ducks came from?" to which the older man instantly replied, "Yes, they just flew down from the Maitai Valley." What a flop that was. It hardly led to a conversation about Creation *or* Christianity!

Witnessing to scientists in the DSIR (Scientific and Industrial Research) was far better done with life than with words. Within a couple of weeks, all the staff knew of my commitment to Christ. I do remember pasting Bible texts on the wall in front of my desk.

Then, as if God had his own mission training programme for me, I received an envelope in the mail marked OHMS. A summons from the New Zealand Army. I'd been balloted into the Territorial Army for 16 weeks of Basic Training. Surprise, surprise, very little personal evangelism took place there, but before the busload of 60 interns had completed the long journey from Nelson to Burnham, Christchurch, they all knew I was a Christian. I was the only one who refused the many visits to the hotel bars, so I was basically the only sober one on the bus.

But my best introduction to personal evangelism, in the context of a local church, came through a coffee bar outreach the youth started on Friday evenings in the Rutherford Street Church. Relationships were formed, and people started studying the Bible together. Coupled with that, Campus Crusade for Christ and Bill Bright's *Four Spiritual Laws* came to town. Teams were trained in a very helpful presentation of the gospel. Little did I know, 20 years later, the connection with Campus Crusade would be renewed. This time preparing the Jesus Film and helping to produce *Ko e Makatuʻunga ʻe Fā ʻo e Moʻui Fakalaumālié* (Four Spiritual Laws), for the Tongan nation.

But here we were now in a small village on the outskirts of Nukuʻalofa, with practically the whole church membership having been born into one of the traditional denominations. Most had a strong familiarity with the Bible's basic storyline but an evident lack of the spiritual dynamic of new birth. The church leadership had already shown a misunderstanding of church-planting, preferring economic advantage for the families over spiritual maturity within the church. Significantly, the congregation itself were a group of dissenters out of nominal denominations. However, God was sovereignly at work within these families. The meaning of The Good News was soon to be experienced one by one as the Lord opened hearts.

The first Sunday morning, January 27, 1974, was dramatic for us. A photograph shows the handful of those present who wanted to be part of this group. The service was vaguely like an Open Brethren, open worship style, as taught by Dr Vic Wilson. Some hymn-singing, along with a few men sharing, but it all meant very little to Colleen and me. We were being inducted into a Tongan church service.

I remember sitting on the front seat, a beautifully varnished wooden form made of Kwila, a hardwood of Papua New Guinea. Bernie had built 12 of these. At the end of the service, I broke down in tears at the realisation that God had led us into this remote setting, far away from familiarity. It might have been the overflow of a few weeks of tension leaving family, but now there was no turning back.

Two weeks after this service, we walked a couple of kilometres down to Queen Salote Wharf to bid farewell to Bernie Tolmie. Now, with no other palangis, we were on our own. Or so we may have thought.

Atenisi and Part-time Teaching

Early in 1974, I visited Professor Futa Helu, the Founder of Atenisi (Athens) Institute, a private secondary school. It was built on the edge of a very low-lying part of Nuku'alofa, with swamp as the main part of the school campus. Buildings were concrete floors and block walls with openings as windows. I offered to make a small contribution to the early beginnings of the school and was immediately presented with an opportunity to teach agricultural science. No formal training required! Just some life experience and desire.

Professor Helu was a radical who challenged the status quo in Tonga and wrote some penetrating articles about social ills:

> Poverty and depravity are increasing... selfishness and avarice have multiplied to such incredible heights as to leave nothing for the needy and the underprivileged, not to mention the frightening rise of crime and all forms of iniquitous behaviour and injustice.[20]

Futa had returned from years of studying at a New Zealand University and wanted to make his own impact via education.

Teaching at Atensi Institute was a significant starting point for me in that it gave a real exposure to levels of poverty not previously experienced. Students sat on a concrete floor, few of them had writing materials, and there were no textbooks to work from.

Professor Helu was very supportive and appreciative of my small participation in his education goals. He was aware we had come as Christian missionaries, yet he was very open to us also running a Saturday night programme for local children as well as students from Gilbert & Ellis Island. Those programmes included singing Christian songs from the Kiwi Ranch songbook and teaching basic Bible lessons.

For several years, about ten students from the Gilbert & Ellis Islands attended church services.

Late in 1975, we became quite exhausted by the pace of life, the heat and stressful issues going on within the Fellowship. We decided that a couple of weeks in Samoa with Betty and Lloyd Brewerton would be refreshing, but we had submitted our passports to the police upon arrival and were waiting for an extension of our three-week Visitor's Visa.

Immigration Authorities were alarmed we were still in the country after two years. They made their own enquiries about what we'd been doing "under the radar" since arriving in 1974.

Professor Helu, unknown to us, had significant influence with government officials. He vouched for our helpful contribution to Tongan society, and along with the thriving kindergarten Colleen had established, our visas were updated so we could safely travel to Samoa for a break.

Colleen Starts a Kindergarten

More then, about the kindergarten. Colleen began to offer support to the children of the community by running a programme two days a week. She quickly got the interest of local families and began to forge good relationships with the mothers. Melenaite Statham, herself a qualified teacher with good English, provided significant help in these early days.

Kindergartens were a totally new thing back then. In many ways, this simple community service gave the church a real presence in the community. New churches, not known to be a part of the establishment, were viewed with some suspicion. However, Colleen's love of children and teaching English was a draw card for local families. Of course, it was also a great place for Colleen to practise her speaking and listening skills as she learned the new language.

Very quickly the numbers reached between 20 and 30 children, with the mothers and caregivers all enjoying the morning experience. Three years later, Princess Pilolevu of the Royal Family established a National Kindergarten Association, in part as a recognition of the Halaleva Kindergarten, as well as the growing interest of families in pre-school education.

Contradicting the Gospel Truth

At the time the Tonga Gospel Fellowship was registered, Christian denominations had been part of Tongan society for over 100 years. Free Wesleyan Church, Free Tonga Church, Anglican, Roman Catholic, and Seventh Day Adventist had established themselves right across the Kingdom. Cults such as Mormons and Jehovah's Witnesses were making aggressive attempts to gain a foothold. At the time of writing, the Baha'i faith, Islam and Hinduism all have small numbers of adherents.

One of my early investigations of the state of Christianity in the Kingdom was to prepare a short set of questions and visit with the leaders of the Christian denominations. The aim was twofold. To introduce myself to these leaders and explain what our focus was going to be. And secondly, to hear what they had to say about the sufficiency of Christ's death for salvation, the assurance of faith, and also issues of mutual respect of each other's ministries.

Not all the leaders warmed to the conversation. One interview however stood out. It was the response of the president of a leading denomination.

The question put was put, "Do you believe it is possible for a Christian to have assurance of eternal life and if so, on what basis?"

He explained that the gift of eternal life was made by God at the end of life based on the good works performed in this life. He said, "God is the final judge and He would weigh up a person's good deeds and bad deeds. Whichever was the greater would determine eternal life or eternal separation."

In other words, no one could be sure of eternal life until the final judgement. Islam offers the same!

I asked if I could read 1 John 5:11-13:

And this is the testimony, that God gave us eternal life, and this life is in his Son. Whoever has the Son has life; whoever does not have the Son of God does not have life. I write these things to you who believe in the name of the Son of God, that you may know that you have eternal life. (1 John 5:11-13)

At the end of reading those verses, the president closed the conversation and politely dismissed me! That conversation came as a shock.

This same sentiment was shared at the first Easter Camp held in the Chapel at Halaleva in 1975. I led two days of studies through Billy Graham's material on Making Disciples. Notes were written out by hand onto paper, with three carbon sheets underneath, producing four copies at a time. That's old-school copying for sure! There was a lot of interest in the camp and the studies since it was a first for the church. Cooking meals together and playing games organised by Torrey, Colleen's brother, all created great memories.

But a much more significant conflict erupted. On the Monday morning, at the end of the camp, participants were asked if they would like to share what they had learned. One man in his late 20s spoke at length and with considerable passion. I asked 'Ofa to give an overview of what was said, since my Tongan was still very limited. 'Ofa relayed to me that according to him, I had made some fundamental errors in my teaching. According to the criticism, salvation was not granted through faith alone, but faith plus works. Aware of the confrontation being presented to the whole group of campers, I responded in a very direct way:

"By grace we are saved through faith, not of ourselves, it is the gift of God. Not of works, so no one should boast." I continued, "There may be many churches that do not teach this truth. Your objection to grace alone by faith alone will not be accepted in the Gospel Fellowship."

In hindsight, that confrontation so early in the life of the church gave us an opportunity to show the distinctiveness of the message we would be teaching. It was almost as if God allowed this objection to highlight the sufficiency of Christ's work for all those who would eventually come to faith. It certainly confirmed that the opinion of the president interviewed earlier was, in fact, the view of a major proportion of church attendees in Tonga.

In 1976, our church was invited to attend a Tonga Bible Society monthly meeting. After recognising representatives of the various denominations, it was quite a shock to be welcomed under the "Other Faiths" along with Mormon and SDA representatives. This again showed the difference in what we were teaching compared to other denominations.

Despite the cautious and conditional recognition of the Tongan Gospel Fellowship by the dominant denominations, an invitation was issued by the Tongan Government for a representative of the Gospel Churches to attend a Land and Church seminar held at the University of South Pacific Centre in 1978. We took this as a positive sign of progress.

Chapter 10

Gospel Living Spreading Wider

Establishment of Believers

The weekly Sunday *lukuluku* (shared food) became a great means of growing community within the young church.

Traditional church feasts, *fakaafe*[21] (celebratory feasting), were a regular part of the traditional churches routine, but there was always a degree of competition amongst the families who put on the feast. Because the families of Gospel Fellowship chose not to segregate or elevate people of high rank or social privilege, our meals had a sense of simplicity about them. Each family brought what they had prepared in their home *umu*[22] and spread it around the whole table.

The leadership strongly encouraged everyone at the church service to remain for the meal. The table tennis table, along with makeshift tables, were set up so everyone could sit around one table. If there wasn't enough room, we'd have two sittings often with 30 to 40 at each sitting. This sharing of what each family could contribute was much more akin to Acts 2, where "they shared our meals with gladness". All the families felt they could share, even out of their meagre contribution.

Another aspect of the traditional *fakaafe* was the system of a priority seating arrangement. The minister/pastor was assigned the head place and descending levels of importance down to the end of the table. Of course, the best food, often a *puaka tunu* (roasted piglet), was placed in front of the most important guests.

Colleen and I, from the start, resisted this tradition by sitting at different parts of the table and deliberately finding a seat away from the head place. This was a little disconcerting for the congregation for a while. However, when the principle of Jesus' servanthood and humility was taught from the Scriptures, it was totally freeing and embraced by the church.

The same principle applied to food preparation. On one occasion, however, I was out watching the fire being set for the *umu*. Wanting to help, I grabbed the axe and began splitting wood. I wasn't sure whether it was a lack of proficiency at splitting or breaking of a *tapu* (Tongan tradition) that the Pastor must never split wood at a feast, but the axe was forcibly removed, and I was told just to sit and watch! Setaleki made sure of that.

Diffusing of the hierarchical structure, however anti-cultural, seemed to play a significant part in uniting and valuing every member of the fellowship. Jesus' washing of the disciples' feet was often used as a prime example. Comments were made at the end of our time in Tonga that one of the deepest lessons learned was that of the servanthood of Jesus Christ among his disciples and how that worked out in a church congregation.

Music and Growth of the Fellowship

It's no secret that wherever a new work of God has begun and thrived, it has been accompanied by gospel-centred, scripturally-inspired music. In Tonga's case, this was largely facilitated by the service of a brilliant Wesleyan Methodist missionary educator-evangelist Dr James Egan Moulton.

He arrived in Tonga in May of 1865 at the request of Tonga's Christian ruler, King George Tupou. At the time, the King lamented that his nominally Christian people were being "destroyed for lack of knowledge." According to the King, although his people were blessed by the work of previous missionaries, they remained largely ignorant of biblical truth. But their hearts and minds were open, and the time was ripe for learning. Moulton's acclaim for ability with language was established when it was recorded he preached his first sermon in Tongan after just three months.[23]

It took us just a few weeks in Tongan church services to recognise tunes from our upbringing. It was probably more than a couple years before we knew enough Tongan to recognise that the tunes were those of the same hymns we had sung. One of the most memorable for them and one of the most popular was that of Philip Bliss' great hymn:

I will sing of my Redeemer
And His wondrous love to me;
On the cruel cross He suffered,
From the curse to set me free.
Sing, oh sing, of my Redeemer,
With His blood, He purchased me.
On the cross, He sealed my pardon,
Paid the debt, and made me free.

Of course, being a Methodist Wesleyan, Moulton had the volumes of Charles Wesley's hymns to draw on as well as those composed by the likes of William Cowper, Dr Lowry and Fanny Crosby. Many of the hymns were written in the time of a "great awakening". It's far beyond the scope of this writing to list the many hymns by CW he translated, sufficient to say there was ample upon which to build the solid foundation that King George had realised was missing. Here is a very short sample:

Holy, Holy, Holy Lord God Almighty; Oh, for a Thousand Tongues to Sing; When I Survey the Wondrous Cross; Behold, Behold the Lamb of God, On the Cross; Shall We Gather at the

River; God Moves in a Mysterious Way; There is a Fountain Filled with Blood; Oh, for a Heart to Praise My God. Follow, Follow, I Will Follow Jesus. Praise God from Whom All Blessings Flow.

Helen Taliai has a catalogue of some 400 Tongan hymns translated from English into the Free Wesleyan Hymn Book, 1826.[24]

John and Charles Wesley's gospel-focused hymns provided a perfect resource for the new generation of believers. This was especially appropriate for the new "Gospel Church" format, where there was a time of the so-called "open worship". Once the weekly remembrance of Christ's death, burial and resurrection became part of the church's tradition, the younger men, particularly, began to use the hymns centred around the beauty and value of Christ as their contribution to worship. This, in turn, led them to search out the scriptures which these hymns had been inspired by. With the new freedom of form that came with the celebration of the Lord's Supper came new ways of corporate worshipping of Christ.

For example, participants in the Lord's Supper would kneel on the concrete floor and sing. A man and sometimes a woman would sing quietly, and soon the congregation joined in. One particularly appropriate hymn was often used, Sankey's "What can wash away my sin, Nothing but the blood of Jesus."

Visiting again in March 2023, after some fifty years, the worshipful praise of Jesus Christ during these services still evoked deep emotion and joy as we joined with our adopted family at the feet of our worthy and wonderful Lord.

Along with this wonderful resource of Tongan hymns provided through the giftedness of those early missionaries, we were introduced to an assortment of newer hymns and new choruses via the Kiwi Ranch Songbook.[25] Who would have thought! For young people newly having found Christ and learning to sing short, simple, memorable choruses in a new language, this was an invigorating change from the traditional music.

He's able, He's able, I know He's able,
I know my Lord is able to carry you through.
He healed the brokenhearted
And set the captive free
He made the lame to walk again
And He gives new life to me.

These songs also became a novel way of learning and pronouncing the English language. Using these songs in Open-Air singing became very popular. Giving personal testimonies, young believers who had experienced some serious rejection from their families were glad to sing "He's able to carry me through". Then, with the swelling of voices and excitement of singing new songs, we called on our language tutor and friend Nigel to help. As usual, he didn't disappoint. Some of the translations he made for the Gospel Fellowship have been recorded and sung over radio and TV in this 21st Century: Jesus keep me near the Cross, When the trumpet of the Lord shall sound, I was sinking deep in sin – Love lifted me, and The Old Rugged Cross are among a few that have made it into the public Gospel repertoire.

This renewal of Gospel preaching and singing appeared to spread across other denominations and spark the creation of new songs using the old themes but with some very different tunes and styles. As with all music, there are many traps that modern trends may fall into. As the lyrics of one insightful modern song aptly put it:

When the music fades,
All is stripped away
And I simply come
Longing just to bring
Something that's of worth...

I'll bring you more than a song,
For a song in itself,
Is not what you've required...

I'm coming back to the heart of worship,
Cos it's all about you,
It's about you Jesus.[26]

In 1985, while we were in New Zealand on an extended furlough, we sold or shared over 300 cassettes of the singing groups that had grown up in the church. With the help in recording of Mr Alan Packer of Christchurch Recording Centre, about 15 songs were recorded. As well as providing some entertainment for our supporters at home, the songs were used repeatedly on the radio broadcasts.

In the period this story records, music became a deeply significant part of the whole picture of Christian discipleship. Growing young believers so they could express the joy of their salvation through music was a very fitting expression of their natural Polynesian style, but even more, an outworking of the Spirit's infilling, "singing and making melody in your hearts unto the Lord" (Ephesians 5:21). Vibrant and creative music is, to this day, an integral part of the Church's life and service.

Much of this new style of music centred on the loveliness of Jesus Christ and the sufficiency of the gospel. During the normal three-to-four-day grieving at family funerals, this music is used, again showing how new worship music has been incorporated into the culture. May God continue to raise up gifted musicians who can merge the theology of past generations with the styles of music in this way.

Tuʻulaki's Conversion and Its Impact

As God was working in the community environment through vibrant new music, he continued to probe even more deeply into the lives of individuals of the older generation. One of the most dramatic conversions was that of Tuʻulaki Afuhaʻamango. She was very influential through her sacrificial hospitality, feeding and often sleeping many of the "Halaleva Gang", of which her boys were leaders. Her home was open to all. At the same time, in her zeal for the old traditions, she provided plenty of opposition to my leadership, particularly around the assurance of salvation apart from good works. However, because of her commitment to reading the scripture, God was able to bring His light into her darkness. This is her story as recalled by her daughters Vaisioa, Mele and Toulini in February 2023.

> Akesa Tuʻutuʻulaki Fanaika Afuhaʻamango was born on 17th of October 1930. She was brought up in the eastern village of Niutoua, Tongatapu. She married Setaleki Mumui Afuhaʻamango from Ōkoa, Vavaʻu. She gives her testimony:
>
> The first gathering of this new group was in Fanga, just outside of Nukuʻalofa. My husband, Setaleki, met with Mr Foster Crane, who was doing missionary work with his wife in Deuba Bible School. Mr Crane visited our island on a Banana Boat.
> Setaleki was on the foreshore selling Tongan handicrafts, which was our livelihood. Seta asked Foster if he would like to buy some of these as memories of his visit to Tonga.
> Foster had a counter proposal – "If I buy these, will you help me with the purpose I have come to Tonga?" So, the

relationship quickly developed. We had already begun to conduct Christian services in our house. In my family, there were nine of us, and then there were Siaosi and Alisi Fatafehi, Fine and Fina Taue, Toni Tuiʻileila, and Jack Tome.

Foster met with us on the first Sunday and began to preach a new message. He said we needed to be individually converted by accepting Jesus Christ into our hearts as our Lord and Saviour. This was a very new teaching to us all. He spoke strongly from the Bible that we needed to be born again. So, by receiving Jesus Christ, we would be given eternal life. Foster explained from the Bible that we could be sure of eternal life now while we were still on earth.

We went with Foster to other villages of Hōfoa and Puke, and our small group had many long discussions about this new teaching. Even though we heard Foster's teaching from the Bible, it seemed impossible to me that eternal life could be received through faith alone, without any works of ours.

At the same time Foster was visiting with us, we were told by the people who owned the land on which we lived that we would have to move off the land. We shared this with Foster, and he agreed to help us find a property to build a church for the Gospel Fellowship.

Setaleki and Fine Taue visited Makaleta ʻUluʻave and asked if she would sell us a piece of land for the new church. She agreed to sell us a property in Halaleva. We gave thanks to God for his grace in giving us land for the church, as well as a place for us to relocate to.

Other European visitors began to come from New Zealand and fellowship with us. They too preached that all people must be born again and that by believing in the death of Jesus Christ, we could know the forgiveness of all our sins. I was very poor at understanding English, so I had to rely on our translators.

Victor Wilson came to work with VSA, and we greatly enjoyed a new church Service called the Breaking of Bread. Soon, because of Foster's planning and the kindness of the Lord, we began to build a church. Bernie Tolmie arrived from New Zealand and together, our small fellowship worked joyfully for a year to complete the building.

Next to arrive were Colleen and Graeme, missionaries from New Zealand. They stayed in the small rooms at the back of the chapel. They learned the Tongan language and taught us the scriptures; we must be born again to belong to the Kingdom of God. Before they learned Tongan, I used to get very angry towards them. Even though I didn't understand much scripture, I was sure heaven was such a wonderful place, I wanted to be there. But I was convinced that I had to try my hardest to be worthy of heaven. How could it possibly be something people could attain without any works at all?

But in January 1976, Graeme did a Bible Study. His subject was "How to be sure you have received Jesus Christ into your life." The study was in Tongan. He showed us Romans 3:23 to convince me that all have sinned and come short of God's holy standard. Then he explained John 3:16, how God so loved the world that He gave His only Son, so whoever believes in Him would not perish but have everlasting life. I realised that this was different from what I believed about working my way to heaven. God had made a way for whoever, for anyone who trusted alone in Jesus Christ. They could receive the promise of eternal life by faith in Jesus Christ.

It was like Jesus Christ was knocking at my heart's door. If I opened my heart to allow Jesus Christ to come and be my Saviour and Lord, I could be born again. It was a great moment to understand this from the scripture.

I returned to our home and asked God to forgive me for trying to do what God had done for me in Jesus Christ. I confessed to God I was a sinner and that I put my faith in Jesus Christ, the Son of God. I opened my heart and received Jesus Christ as my Lord and Saviour. Scripture became real to me.

> And this is the testimony, that God gave us eternal life, and this life is in his Son. Whoever has the Son has life; whoever does not have the Son of God does not have life. (1 John 5:11,12)

Praise God, He was patient with me and gave me this wonderful opportunity to be blessed with eternal life. It wasn't any of my good works that could take me to heaven, but the work of Jesus Christ on the cross. He took my place. He carried my sins and died instead of me. He rose again to prove He was the Son of God. His victory over death paid for all my sins. It was His love for me that gave me the right to eternal life now and a dwelling place in heaven with Him for eternity.[27]

From our perspective, as the only resident missionaries, the conversion of Tu'ulaki was not only an inspiration; she had been a frightening opponent of the message of God's grace and seemed to have some influential people around her, but her decisive conversion was testimony to the grace of God, no matter how hard the heart. Remember Saul of Tarsus?

As wonderful as Tuʻulaki's conversion was, in terms of being one of the first real adult supporters of the mission, she quickly became the backbone of the Fellowship. She was a catalyst for the newly-converted youth to be bold about their faith. Her passion for God certainly impacted the older members, and she quickly became a precious friend, even a Tongan mother to our small family.

Tuʻulaki's most significant contribution was this: though they lived basically on a subsistence level, she somehow always had food available at her place. She often made a meal for her family of 12 stretch to 20 or more. She became our strongest encourager of youth night programmes and the Sunday evening variety programmes. Many days I can remember turning up at her very basic home, two large sleeping rooms and an outside kitchen. I was warmly invited to share a large *kulo* (pot) of soup and manioke. "*Haʻu ʻo kai*" (Come, let's eat), and after being a little tentative to start, was quickly at ease and didn't have to be asked twice.

Colleen learned to do the same when the same group of boys came walking past our home on their way home from school. Only eternity will reveal just how much influence Tuʻulaki had on the establishment of the Gospel Churches in Tonga. She was 100 percent committed to preaching that the only way to salvation was by grace and faith alone, not the fulfilling of religious duties or making the yearly *misinale* (missionary offering).[28]

Top: Halaleva Opening. December 1973. Left to right: Fine Taue, Foster Crane, Victor Wilson, Sione Lalahi, Bernie Tolmie.
Bottom: Communion December 1973. Left to right, standing: Fine, Siaosi, Saia, Unga, Paula. Middle: Mele, Bernie, Unknown, Pila, Samiuela, Tulaki. Front: Toulini, Leimoni, Sione, Fepaki, Fololita, Moeaki, Victor Wilson, Sione, 'Ofa, Margret (Canadian volunteer).

Top: *First Coral Coast Bible students.*
Left to right: Paula Afuhaʻamango, ʻOfa Fatafehi, Limi Hai, Samiuela Tukipili, Saia Unufe. Bottom: *Our first faletonga at Halaleva.*

Top: Joel, Janita and Gene ready for school in the 1980s.
Bottom: Our earliest congregation, February 1974.

Top left: Tuʻulaki painting tapaʻingatu, one of her traditional skills. Right: Colleen and Etuini praying at kindy. Bottom: Colleen with her first team of kindergarten teachers.

Photos | 125

Top: 'Ofa preaching at one of the many open air meetings.
Bottom: Graeme preaching at the annual agriculture show using
the Sowers Portable platform and picture board.

Top: Tali baptising Timote. Bottom: Graeme preaching at A3Z radio station – The Gospel Half Hour.

Top: Our first radio singing group, with Hammond organ and marimba. Left to right: Colleen, 'Ofa, Saia, Esafe, Tali, Naisa, Inoke. Bottom: Penaia and Setaleki providing entertainment.

128 | *Fangufangu Mana*

Top: The Halaleva "Fab Four". Bottom: Prisoners in Hu'atolitoli returning to cells following our church programme.

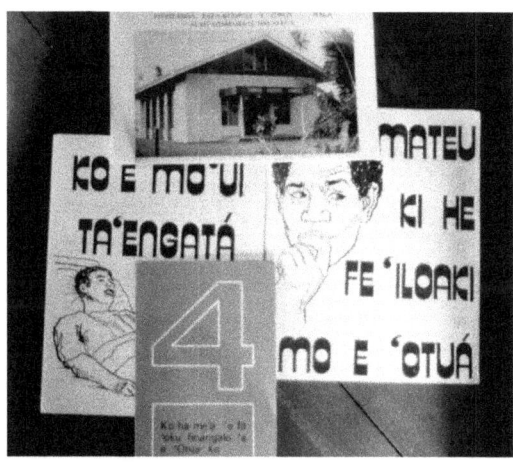

Top: Tracts distributed to every village on Tongatapu, 1977.
Bottom: One of the tract visitation teams. Left to right: Inoke, 'Ofa,
Fine, Vaisioa, Naisa, Mele Kaloni.

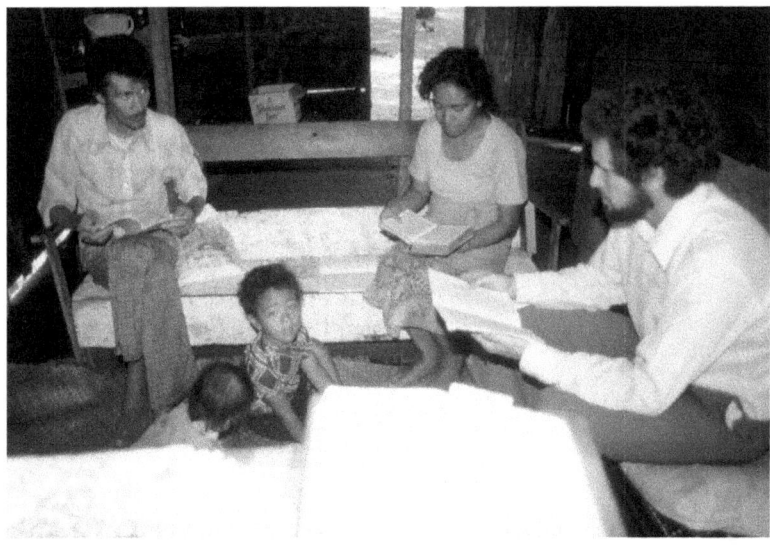

Top: *Siaosi and Neta Sandys, Nehemaia and Mele, at a home Bible study with Graeme. Bottom: Esafe leading the youth choir.*

Photos | 131

Top: One of the GLO teams training with local Christians at the Touliki church-plant. Bottom: Rowland and Elaine Foreman with Charles Erlam. A GLO team going on an island picnic.

Top: One of the first visits to Vavaʻu. Back: Inoke, Isei, Naisa. Front: ʻOfa Mele, Graeme. Bottom: The Leimatuʻa congregation, 1985.

Top: Ongolea Kavamoʻungaone Family. Back: Fei, Ilima, Ongolea lahi, Naomi, Fusi, Sione, Ongolea siʻi, Faiva. Front: Kala, Tuʻi, Filipe, Isaia, Maʻata. Bottom: Kalesita in Houma with a cassette player from CRC Christchurch.

Top: Visiting villages in Vava'u. Fifita and Meliame on foot, Penitoa and Joel on horseback. Bottom: A graduating class of TEE Study Discipleship.

Photos | 135

Top: Touliki congregation outside the first building made from on-site coconut timber. Bottom: Atunaisa and Manu Ngalu, pastor teacher from 1988 to present.

*Polynesian Workers' Conference, Coral Coast Fiji, 1978.
Left to right, back row: Samuels, Foster Crane, Naisa Ngalu,
Will Crampton, Ene Sagala, Graeme McNae, Alan Packer.
Middle row: Rita Samuels, Lili'a Sagala, Ngaire Scott,
Ruth Alexander, Gwen Crane, Ernie Edwards, Colleen McNae.
Front row: Michael Dutta, Ike Samuels, wife,
'Ofa Fatafehi and Janita, Lloyd Brewerton.*

Chapter 11

Women and Children

Alongside the direct evangelical activities of the mission was the strategic community involvement with women and children. Colleen had the skills and passion to initiate this, and writes this chapter about the ministries she contributed to.

I (Colleen) had the privilege of working alongside hard-working, clued-up, intelligent women for more than 15 years. They knew how to weave walls for a house and roof, cook great meals on very primitive forms of heating (mainly an open fire), weave mats and make *tapaingatu* (tapa cloth), keep a house tidy and sweep the yard, wash clothes and provide nurture for their children. That was the main role of women.

That was when we first went to Tonga. Things are sure different in these modern days. As time went on and girls had opportunities to go to university after completing high school, with the education they received, they could get good jobs and really contribute to family finances.

My main ministry has always been in my home with my husband and children, who were central to my life. I took it seriously to train and teach the children biblical principles and how to be kind, gentle, fun, thoughtful and truthful. As the years went by, young married couples noticed how differently we related to our children and how differently they behaved during church services. We had many meaningful conversations with these young families and some of them adopted many of our routines in running the household.

Establishing the Pre-school

In those early days, with a goal of bringing the Good News of faith in Christ and the accompanying new life, we prayed about what ways we could reach out to help our community in Halaleva. There were a few pre-schools running in Tonga. Princess Pilolevu was a great advocate and promoted pre-school education, so I went along to a couple of workshop days in Tonga and also signed up through Wellington University to do a course in Early Childhood Education.

We started the pre-school in early 1975, once we had a bit of equipment. We built a climber, swings made from old tyres, and a sand pit. Also, we had a few puzzles and toys to play with.

One of the young ladies in the church, with vision and great gentleness, Vaisioa Afuha'amango, helped that first year, and it was really rewarding, especially in terms of discipleship training which worked both ways. I did most of the teaching in English, with a few Tongan words splattered here and there. Vaisioa developed in her passion for children and ability to teach them. We often prayed together and developed a close friendship in the context of Christian service.

Parents liked their children to be educated in English as eventually they may get into Tonga High School, which was the cream of Tongan secondary schools. Parents were very open to the Christian teaching we did.

We started each day with prayer, teaching them simple bilingual Christian songs they all enjoyed. I developed a syllabus of learning goals each year, and we went for it. I loved those pre-school children. They were so quick to learn and so coordinated when it came to ball throwing. Some showed amazing painting skills for their age. We included field trips to parks and beaches nearby. At the end of the year, we had a very ornate prize giving where all the children were dressed in beautiful party clothes. They did action games and dances that really impressed the parents. It was amazing to see the large crowd of extended families attending.

And so, the word spread of the value of the Gospel Fellowship to the community. Vaisioa and I were deeply satisfied with the impact we could have on these precious lives.

The preschool ran for 11 years. Through it, we made a lot of friends and really helped to put Tonga Gospel Fellowship on the map, especially in our immediate district. We became an authentic and valued part of the community.

One lady who lived out the back of the church, with no strong denominational following, began to attend out of mere curiosity. Susi and I became close friends and still are to this day. She brought her children to preschool and joined in the socialising that went with it. Her son, Etuini, was very cute and would often say prayers for us.

One day, I was telling the children a Bible story and mentioned that the Bible was God's important book of instructions for us and that it would be good if we all had a Bible at home and read it. Etuini went home and told Susi and Uhila they must get a Bible and read it because *Kolini* (Colleen) said so.

After many years of this close friendship, I offered to take Susi through a simple outline of the Christian gospel. She committed her life to Jesus Christ and began to faithfully attend church worship.

Second-Hand Clothes

Dear Mrs Queenie Hewlett from Auckland was a wonderful helper to our mission. She gathered second-hand clothes and packed them very tightly and proficiently in tea chests and sent them four at a time to us in Tonga. In those days, there were very few clothes to buy anywhere in town. The small selection of what new clothes there were, were expensive and few could afford them. Fabric was available, but very few local ladies had sewing machines, so cheap second-hand clothes were a great help.

It was somewhat of a surprise how every Sunday, the ladies who attended church were so beautifully dressed. They were great at colour coordination and style and had high personal pride. I had to pick up my dress standard when we got to Tonga. Tongan women seem to have an innate ability to prepare themselves with grace and elegance.

Emptying the tea chest of clothes onto the ping-pong room floor, we would staple a price on each article of clothing. That was always fun, and especially when we had visitors from New Zealand staying with us.

A girlfriend of mine was with us at one stage and helped me to mark the clothes. We pulled out one outfit from the tea chest and straight away recognised it. A very nicely dressed lady in our home church in Rotorua had worn it for a summer and always looked exquisite. Matching high-heeled shoes and a hat came with it. We priced it cheap, and it sold quickly. The next day at church, a dear lady walked in with this same outfit on but no shoes, no bra and only a few teeth. My friend and I disgraced ourselves with our outburst of laughter. But it was always a great day when we spread out a *tāpolini* (tarpaulin) and then covered it with the price-marked clothes. The money received went back into church projects for the overall ministry.

The faithfulness and humility of the ladies at all the church gatherings was amazing. They always looked immaculate in appearance but always with a heart to learn and serve. We had camps together in one of our homes with full-on Bible studies;

they took charge of the meals. At Easter, all the ladies worked tirelessly to cook for upwards of 100 campers. Tongan *keke* (round donuts) for breakfast, with bread and buns and tea or Milo. Then in later years, eggs and bacon, sausages, root crops and more. Lunch was usually such a feast, with all the trimmings. When the Afuhaʻamango family moved to America, they would send plastic plates and cups along with money to help pay for food. I grew to love my Tongan sisters more and more every year.

Sewing Classes

Being a keen seamstress, I took my electric sewing machine to Tonga, but with few people owning machines or even having electricity, it was no use. After our first furlough to New Zealand in April 1977, we procured two treadle sewing machines with which to start sewing classes.

The ladies in our community were very interested to learn. I got to know them more when we did our weekly class. Bible study first, then we'd get on to sewing. I would go in the Datsun van at about 12.30 to pick up ladies from far villages, and we'd start at about 2.00. The mature ladies from the church would help with the Bible studies. I would prepare about once every six weeks as it had to be in Tongan, which was quite a challenge for me. I could have an ordinary conversation, but to have all the Biblical vocabulary was another large step which I never made well.

Sometimes, the ladies would bring their own fabric to sew. I had a few patterns which I had brought over from home And showed them how to use them. Because patterns were not available in Tonga, ladies would just lay another garment over the fabric and cut around it. It amazed me how skilful they were, but they had basic skills using patterns from making tapa cloth. Their efforts usually turned out very well.

At the start, we only had a couple of machines, so we had to share them all the time. We really needed more, so I put the word out to the churches in New Zealand. A group of ladies from the Browns Bay Assembly found 12 unused treadle machines from donors. But how to get them over?

God always has a way, even for menial issues like this. Someone in the Browns Bay Christian community heard that there was an air force Hercules making an official flight to Tonga and that there was room for the cargo if it was for a charitable cause. After gaining permission from the authorities, the machines were loaded aboard. Graeme and I went out to Fuaʻamotu Airport to take delivery. I won't forget this great big thing rumbling and coughing its way down the runway and thought, how marvellous are God's ways. We kept some for the sewing class and distributed others to faithful ladies in the group, but not without some gossip and criticism around the choosing of who got and who didn't get. Familiar? Things don't change down the years, such is the human heart.

Tuʻulaki had a friend, Alamita, whom she invited to the sewing class. Alamita had a successful business selling a wide range of Tongan handcrafts at the Talamahu Market Centre. She enjoyed the sewing class and became an integral part of the ladies' group. She made a significant contribution to the group through her craft skills as well as her deep interest in the spiritual well-being of the women.

After a few weeks, Alamita, her husband Semisi and their six children started attending Tonga Gospel Fellowship with us. Nui, Liueli, Alilia, Toulini, Isei and Aisea were a welcomed addition to the fellowship. They all joined the life of the church and played a significant role in the open-airs each Sunday. All this was a flow on benefit of the sewing class.

One year (1981), as a result of material scraps sent over by our dear Queenie Hewlett, we decided to upskill our sewing class by offering a quilting class. This involved another level of precision, which these clever ladies were prepared for. Large scraps of fabric were sent in the tea chests from Auckland and Rotorua, and we ended up with quite an amazing selection.

The class's colour coordination and ideas were spectacular, and some of the quilts were quite exquisite. We've included a picture of the prizegiving day. Since, at the time, quilting was quite an innovation for Tongan ladies, we decided to show their work, a Tongan version of a "Wearable Art" show. Helen Taliai, wife of the well-known principal and church leader, Siupeli, was invited to judge and award the prizes.

It was a great day. We displayed the quilts on make-shift lines around the church grounds. They were a fabulous display of the skill and creativity of Tongan women, a very real testimony to the creativity God has put in each of us. Afternoon tea was served, after which we gave thanks to God for many aspects of the quilting class.

Chapter 12

The Word and Witness

Bible Studies

From the earliest days of the mission, weekly home Bible studies were a regular part of the church family. Of course, family devotions, both morning and evening, have been part of most homes since the early years of Christian mission. These were mostly led by the parents. Often, however, according to those who have experienced spiritual renewal, these devotions are very ritualistic. Little meaningful teaching of scripture or purposeful prayer involving participation was offered. Some of the traditional churches used the ancient method of Catechism learning.[29] That was their typical Sunday School format.

Because our congregation was scattered across many villages within Nukuʻalofa, without any means of transport, we began to offer home Bible studies three nights a week. This was a lot of work and meant nights of the week away from home. However, it was an invaluable means of connecting on a very personal basis with the key families. One of the reasons this played such a significant part in establishing the church was the interactive way of teaching scripture, instead of a monologue from either parent. All the family were involved in singing popular songs and traditional hymns. We could also involve children in prayers together with the whole family. Many families enjoyed the new format so much, they would invite neighbours to join.

Pastoral care, too, was naturally offered in the home setting. A Tongan system of communication, *talatala'ifale* (in-house conversation), was brought into the realm of learning to walk with God in a more private setting, including face-to-face discussion of the scriptures (Acts 2:41,42). This was an innovative approach to spiritual nurturing that was not practised in traditional denominations. Leaders were taught how to explain the scriptures in small group settings and how to involve family units in these home studies.

Your word is a lamp to my feet and a light to my path. (Psalm 119:105)

Blessed is the man whose... delight is in the law of the Lord, and on his law he meditates day and night. (Psalm 1:1,2)

From a purely social aspect, Colleen and I developed strong bonds with those we visited, and a deep respect and love grew for the families. This means of gathering around the scriptures enabled us to reach out to other villages and to relative strangers. The home Bible studies were an extremely transferable strategy of evangelism and nurturing of new and growing believers.

Easter Camps

One of the annual highlights of church life began when we introduced the Easter Camp. This was an innovation fostering fellowship over an extended weekend. It proved to be inspiring for the newly-forming congregation, giving opportunity for participation. New contacts were made, and over time, many became committed members after their conversions. For the first decade, Easter Camps were held at the Halaleva property.

Colleen and I had both been exposed to the benefits of Christian camping. We had first met and began our courtship in the late 1960s at Mount Maunganui Bible Class Camp. Colleen had been at the heart of the growth and development of the Kiwi Ranch camping mission. No surprise then that as soon as a reasonable number of families had begun to regularly attend Sunday services and Bible studies during the week, we'd ask the question, "Would church camps be appropriate in Tongan culture?"

At the first overnight camp five youth joined Nigel and I for a sleepover at Anahulu Beach. We had drawn a basic picture of the Old Testament Tabernacle as it was a helpful picture of the way of salvation in the New Testament. I recall having at least three sessions. Downtime was swimming in the beautiful lagoon and going for *lanu* (wash down) in the fresh-water pool in the cave. This small "experiment" was accepted enthusiastically by the youth and their parents.

When Easter 1975 came around, and we had settled somewhat after the initial challenges of climate and language, we said, "Let's do this!" However, we needed some serious modifications to the New Zealand format.

At first, the church purchased the supplies for a basic menu. The women were great at making Tongan doughnuts (*keke*) and *tōpai* (a flour, sugar and coconut mix). With an abundance of papaya (*lesi*), mangoes, and citrus fruits like lime, oranges and mandarins, breakfast was easily sorted. Tongan biscuits – *mā pakupaku* – otherwise called "Cabin Crackers", were delicious, especially if they were dunked into tea.

The main meal was a lot more intensive, however. An abundance of root crops – talo, kumala, manioke and yam – for starters. Then the staple mutton flaps, a Kiwi "throw-away" plus the legendary *tunu puaka* (BBQ pig), and whatever variety of fish the local fisherman provided.

The positive for cooking was the community effort involved in putting it all together. Crockery and cutlery were another story. At our earliest camp, we used improvised plates, large breadfruit leaves. They were as rigid as the modern flimsy plastics – no problem with washing dishes, just disposable organics! From memory, cutlery was sent up in the tea chests. Outdoor fires and the underground *umu* required a lot of firewood.

The organisation of such an event provided another opportunity for cooperation. This was a very easy way of involving fringe families and friends in working together. Easter camps were extremely helpful for relationship building. It was rare to have a weekend together like this without new families joining regular Sunday morning services.

Sleeping arrangements presented a serious and sensitive cultural challenge. There is a strict separation of teenage girls and boys in the home setting. So, in consultation with the parents, one or two large tents were erected for the boys, while the girls slept in the ping-pong room or even in the chapel itself. This meant it was necessary for parents to attend the whole programme and sleep with their children.

In Tongan family tradition, prayers are offered morning and night, so devotional times in the tents were arranged and shared around the campers. This gave more opportunity for new Christians to participate.

The worship and teaching sessions were usually 9–11 a.m., 2–4 p.m. and 7–9 p.m. The evening session was where the gospel-centred impact was at its greatest. In the years we were serving, I would choose themes from the Gospels, Romans and Ephesians, as well as Old Testament themes including studies from Exodus, Joshua and Nehemiah. The benefit of this was that the young generation of men grew not just in the scriptures, of which they were quite familiar, but more in how these themes were interpreted in the context of the death, burial and resurrection of Jesus – the heart of the gospel. Many of these young men were soon capable of taking teaching sessions and evangelistic talks in the evenings.

The Saturday evening programme quickly grew into a time when different groups presented songs. Families first, when numbers were small, and then quartets, choirs, and smaller groups from their different villages as Easter camp became more popular. Many Saturday and Sunday afternoons were used for visitation to invite neighbours in. Some Saturday afternoons, we had team competitions of multisport activities. The church property was perfect for this.

Sunday evening became a camp finale, including drama, musical items, testimonies, and a final sermon calling for conversion. Often, we presented a summary message of the camp theme. As people responded to an appeal to follow Christ, new Christians were given the opportunity to develop the skill of counselling for salvation. Of course, there was a supper to follow, consisting of the leftover Sunday lunch and some more Tongan *keke*.

Monday morning was a reflection time when the "floor was opened" for any who wanted to give testimony to the blessing of Easter Camp. Often, visiting campers spoke of their first-time commitment to Christ. Some would testify to the newness of the teaching and their desire to make this their preferred church, a significant opportunity in a heavily denominationalised community.

Over the 15 years of camping, visiting speakers from overseas became a wonderful opportunity to invite teachers from our Pacific Island neighbours. This, in turn, gave the new church movement a real sense of belonging to an international body of Jesus followers outside of the smallness and isolation of our tiny nation.

Some of the speakers included Maika Bovoro, Penaia Samosamovondre, Michael Dutta, Foster and Gwen Crane, Brian Stokes from Fiji, Rowland and Elaine Forman, Bruce and Sue Reid, Herb and Ngaire Ritchie, Dr Sam Martin, and even Jim and Agnes Boswell from Canada.

It would be hard to overstate the value of Easter Camps and the impact on the health and well-being of the whole movement of Gospel Churches. Memories abound of the lessons of spiritual growth. And there was a lot of fun. I'll never forget the look on Tuʻulaki's face when, during a big clean-up on the last day, I emptied a bucket of water over her. The floodgates opened as everybody joined in – unheard of at a Christian camp until then.

The fact that Easter Camps have continued unabated for the ensuing 35 years after our return is evidence of their contribution to church life. Camps are now being held in the Leimatuʻa church, Vavaʻu.

Theological Education by Extension (TEE)

One of the non-negotiable foundations of a long-term church-based mission is the faithful, consecutive teaching of the whole counsel of God. From Paul revisiting the churches in Asia Minor in Acts to the Cave Churches in Goreme, Cappadocia, of the Fourth Century, through the Dark Ages and then the Reformation of the 17th Century, consistent teaching of the Word of God to the people of God has continually given the scriptures the highest place and the Lord Jesus Christ the place of highest honour.

I was reminded by one of the young leaders some years after returning from Tonga that it was the weekly home Bible Studies that set the foundation for the church. The "main thing" of church life was the glory of God in Christ as declared through the scriptures. Other activities, such as, music competitions and sporting events as a means of attempting to keep the church relevant, were less important.

It was a providential then that the Christian Leaders' Training College (CLTC), based in Papua New Guinea, made contact. Ian Malins had prepared several courses for second-language English speakers and made them available to Tonga. Shipping the books was a bit of a problem, but having a contact at the post office was always helpful. (Remember the postmaster and watermelon story?) In 1983, 20 course books and a leaders' guide arrived. The first course was called "Come Follow Me", a 12-lesson course on discipleship, taken from the four Gospels.

Word spread around the Christian community, and others from a group in town under the leadership of Losena Fatai soon joined. They were the "zealots" of the Campus Crusade team. This was the beginning of several courses that continued until 1988.

The discipleship course was particularly useful in that it set out sequentially and powerfully the principles of following Jesus Christ. Students were required to study the assigned passages from the Gospels. They had to fill in the blanks of the notes in their manuals. Finally, they were required to complete a two-page test, which was handed in for marking, including writing out each week's memory verse. The value of this course was recognised by the young leaders. A small team headed up by Naisa and 'Ofa Tafa set about translating and reproducing the discipleship course in Tongan. This was used for many years by the churches following our return to New Zealand.

Besides this very valuable course, the TEE studies continued with further themes; 1 and 2 Corinthians, Ephesians, and Christian Worship. This was the first experience of formal theological learning for people gathering at the Fellowship. TEE studies made a significant contribution to the establishment of the mission.

It was very affordable for all students. It was a challenge for some, having to read the English notes, but hearing the weekly teaching in Tongan was a perfect compliment. Also, the studies took place in the environment of the local church. Being a very communally-based society, they thrived in this learning environment. In contrast to the traditional sermons, where congregations were preached "down to", this was refreshing and invigorating. Question and answer times were part of the weekly study, so participation in the learning was also a very new experience for everyone. The group accountability provided momentum for students to persevere.

The Jesus Film

In the 1970s, Bill Bright of Campus Crusade for Christ (CCC) had a vision to prepare a film about the life of Christ using Luke's Gospel as the script. He wanted it screened in as many countries in the world as possible. The script was to be presented in the local language and dubbed over the English version. Tonga, being one of the smallest countries in the world, was chosen as a trial for training and logistical purposes.

In 1979, under the leadership of Wes Brenemann, CCC brought a delegation to Tonga and made a proposal to the Christian church leaders. The gathering was held at the Dateline Hotel with the prime minister, Prince Fatafehi Tuʻipelehake, himself a keen Christian, in attendance. Wes made a compelling presentation, creating the vision and asking for a response from the churches. All he got was Silence!

I was excited and saw the potential for evangelising with other churches. Since no other church leaders spoke up, I expressed my personal enthusiasm for the project. Another silence, possibly because the Prime Minister was in attendance. He then addressed the group positively and suggested that the palangi, who was so keen, be part of a steering committee. Eventually, Isi Taukolo (Pentecostal), Alifeleti Mone (FWC), Kelepi Mailau (Navigators) and Losena Fatai (CCC) all agreed to work together.

So, the plan developed. Nigel Statham, who was working

with CCC and Scripture Union, was approached to help with the production of written material as well as coordination of the recordings. A lot of work went into selecting appropriate voices for the characters. A police magistrate, Ti'o, had a deep and somewhat sinister voice, so he was selected as the Devil's voice and did a great job. After a couple of months of recording and syncing those recordings with the characters in the film, recordings were made with the help of A3Z recording studios. These were sent away and dubbed over the original soundtrack, and the film was ready for showing across the Kingdom.

A Premiere showing was made to invited guests at Hauhau 'o Taufa'ahau Theatre, at which His Majesty King Taufa'ahau Tupou IV and Queen Halaevalu Mata'aho 'Ahome'e graced us with their presence. Nigel Statham was the MC and performed his duties with fear and trepidation. The evening began and concluded with the Police Band playing the Tongan National anthem. This is standard protocol for all events in the presence of the reigning monarch, but added a sense that this was a national and interdenominational vision. A thrilling endeavour, presenting the gospel in a completely new form.

The essential work then began; training teams of volunteers from many churches to take a generator, projector, screen, sound system, and power cables and set up at each of the venues across the nation. The Gethsemane Youth Groups, along with the Gospel Youth, were disproportionately represented in these teams and provided the backbone of the project. Losena Fatai was responsible for the training of counsellors for those who enquired for more information about making a commitment to Christ.

The target was to show the film at least once in every village on every one of the 36 inhabited islands. Teams worked their way across all the villages on Tongatapu. Showings were done in the open spaces as well as in church and public halls. Preference was given to community halls, so all felt free to attend. The police superintendent of the time, Paula Vivili, offered invaluable support. He was highly respected. He took responsibility for the security and safety of the teams but also added a degree of confidence for the general public. An interdenominational project was often viewed with some suspicion as a subtle attempt to establish break-away groups from the traditional churches. It was very helpful to have different representatives from different churches introducing and closing the showing of the film.

After the initial showings, Losena Fatai and Melenaite Statham, along with the youth from Gethsemane, offered an ongoing support programme to all the villages that had serious enquirers. This was called *"Tanumaki"* – a gardening term for mounding up good soil around the root system of growing plants.

But how could we get a team of trained evangelists along with a generator, projector, and accessories onto remote islands? Many of them had no wharf and were encircled by systems of reefs. Well, where it is God's will, there will always be a way. We enlisted the experience of many who had grown up on these islands and mastered their reefs and wharves. Enter a beautiful yacht, *Providence*, from Tauranga. A team including Kelepi Mailau, 'Ofa Fatafehi and I sailed from Nuku'alofa on November 3rd and visited nine of these tiny islands. There were 13 screenings, some in darkened buildings in daytime, to approximately 4,000 people. Some 400 people were counselled, wanting to know more about knowing Jesus Christ as a personal Saviour. The team experienced typically overwhelming Tongan hospitality.

Similarly, teams of which I was a part used local vessels to visit all the inhabited islands in the maze of the Vava'u group. The map will show what a massive task this was.

Then a unique opportunity presented itself, as a government vessel was making a trip to Tonga's northernmost island,

Niuatoputapu, otherwise known as Tin Can Island. It inherited this name since mail from passing vessels was dropped off in a tin can and a swimmer would come out and replace it with the tin of outgoing mail. Since the film team had to carry a generator and film projector, it was decided this was the perfect opportunity to show the film on Niuatoputapu A team of five of us took the journey in March of 1981. It was unforgettable.

We left Neiafu Harbour, Vava'u, in quiet seas, arriving off the coast of Niuatoputapu some 18 hours later. The island is an active volcano without any beaches or wharves. Getting off the vessel and onto land wasn't for the fainthearted.

The wooden vessel was loosely tied up in deep water next to a rocky ledge. Passengers were told the precise moment amidst the surging of the tide, to jump onto the rocky ledge. Yeah right! Plenty of locals were on hand to rescue those who missed.

However, for those who travelled "business class", which included the Minister of Land, his dignitaries and me, the palangi (a church minister and all), there was a much more predictable method of getting ashore. We were let down off the ferry into what looked like a genuine lifeboat, with seats for about a dozen. Two men had paddled a local canoe out with a large rope and attached it to the bow of our lifeboat.

We rowed slowly toward the volcanic shingle shoreline but waited at least 50 metres out, just before the wave break. At the appropriate time in the cycle of the waves, somewhat like a surfer waiting for his moment, a team of 30 or so guys on shore yelled, "*Toho!*" which means pull, pull hard-out! When our boat hit the steep gravel shoreline, another team of men ran towards our boat. While we were being pulled up the beach, another group literally lifted it out of the water and away from the beachline. Yes, people and all, out of the sea and carried us, free of the surf, to dry land. We all got out without getting our feet wet. Yep, unforgettable!

There were two showings of the Jesus Film, with around a hundred viewers at each. People were honestly aghast to hear the amazing story of the Life of Christ in their own language. Many people talked with the CCC team after hearing an appeal to put personal faith in Christ. As is always the case, following up people with an interest in following Christ after these presentations was a huge undertaking. Many possessed a Bible, and since it is God who brings about new life, we're confident He will have preserved His own children.

Some memorable events must be shared during the three nights we stayed on Niuatoputapu. The first was being led into the densely forested parts by a crowd of children and a couple of adult guides. The kids were quickly breaking open fallen logs and retrieving the 'ofato grubs, not dissimilar to New Zealand's huhu grubs. The kids were eating them raw, so the team joined in for this rare opportunity. Can't say I'd recommend the grubs for a normal diet.

Another unique opportunity was looking for the eggs of a bird native to the Niuas, the Malau Incubator Bird. This rare bird lays its eggs in uncompacted volcanic soil near active steam vents. The natural warmth of the soil takes the place of incubation, otherwise provided by the mother. Locals love to eat these eggs. We looked, but unfortunately for us, had no luck. But the most pleasurable of these events was to swim in the freshwater pools of Hihifo.

Paula Vivili

One of the sadder records associated with the Jesus Film Project was that of Paula Vivili mentioned earlier. He was asked by Losena Fatai, a close friend, if he would help with the interisland logistics, transportation and communications throughout the many islands. He was Superintendent of Police at the time of the Jesus

Film Project and the ideal person for the multiple tasks. Paula was greatly supportive of this interdenominational project.

I was in regular communication with Losena because of our mutual passion to teach the gospel truth wherever we could. On one occasion, I asked Losena if she had been in touch with Paula. Losena, with deep concern, asked if I would please visit Paula to support him in some serious domestic issues he was having. She said she didn't know anyone else who might be able to offer much-needed support and counsel.

I was very hesitant to get involved, not knowing him well enough for such a delicate issue. As well, his seniority within the community was a little like the Apostle Paul being summoned to speak with King Agrippa. However, Losena persisted, as she often did out of her passion for people's spiritual well-being. I conceded by saying I would pray, and if I met with him at some time, would take it from the Lord that he had arranged our meeting.

Some months later, as I was finishing a radio broadcast, there he was coming down the passageway outside the recording studio! He was very warm as we exchanged pleasantries, but I suddenly realised this was the moment I'd been praying about. So I asked for a chance to catch up. Paula was very open to the suggestion and proposed a meeting for Tuesday afternoon of the following week. He explained he was flying out to Niuatoputapu on Wednesday.

I arrived at his office at BP Oil. He was the manager of the large petroleum company and worked from a second-floor office of the Maʻofanga Business Centre, overlooking Queen Salote Wharf. After welcoming me, Paula spoke across his large desk with the familiar words, "What brings you here today?"

I explained I had come as a friend but that I had also heard confidentially from one of his close friends that there may be some difficult domestic issues he was facing. Silence!

Slowly, Paula looked up directly at me and said, "I've got lots of responsibilities and authority in the community. This is a very sensitive and potentially dangerous issue you have raised. Are you not aware this could cause you serious personal harm?"

I was shocked and felt rather intimidated. "Paula," I said, "I have prayed about this conversation for quite a few months, and when we met at A3Z last week, I took it as an answer to prayer. I've come as a representative of Jesus Christ with a desire to show love and concern for you, my friend."

Another silence! Paula then looked up, but this time with tears coming down his broad cheek.

"I thank you, Graeme. Of all the people God could have used to speak with me about my problem, it had to be a palangi. Not one of my church congregation or its leaders, but a palangi."

It was a tense, emotional moment. Paula's demeanour changed from defensiveness to open humility and sorrow. We spoke for some time about how Christians can walk with God through trials. He was obviously deeply moved and explained that he sincerely wanted to continue the conversation but had urgent business to attend to since he was flying in a couple of days. He invited me to come again and that he would call when he returned to make the arrangement.

The flight left Tongatapu on the 90-minute journey, with five passengers. On preparation to land in Niuatoputapu, however, the captain reported a problem with the front wheel landing gear. A decision was made to return to Tongatapu and make an emergency landing. There would be plenty of services available for this. As they neared Fua'amotu Airport, the captain jettisoned the fuel and came in for what was expected to be a belly landing. Scary, but regarded as relatively safe for experienced pilots. On impact, however, the plane flipped onto its back with ensuing chaos.

Four passengers and the captain survived the crash landing, but Paula was tragically killed.[30] This happened in April 1983.

I was deeply impacted by this tragedy, as was the whole of Tonga. I was grateful for the opportunity to speak of God's love and truth into a friend's life in a time of need. God can use us all in moments like this. It's our availability, but His wisdom and grace. "Shall not the judge of all the earth do right?" (Genesis 18:25) Surely this is another example of the wonderful sound of the gospel reaching into the hearts of men who are awakened to listen.

Look carefully then how you walk, not as unwise but as wise, making the best use of the time... (Ephesians 5:16)

Chapter 13

Open-Air Evangelism

Within a year of the formal commencement of services in the Halaleva church building, attempts had begun to preach the gospel on street corners in Nuku'alofa.

My only previous experience with open-air evangelism was holding a placard on Trafalgar Street, Nelson, on Friday nights, while a couple of older men held forth on the serious themes of sin, salvation and judgement. A very intimidating experience for listeners, to say nothing of the fear of a young Christian standing with these battle-hardened, no-compromise preachers.

Open-air style evangelism was virtually non-existent in Tonga in the seventies. It was not part of traditional churches activity since 90 percent of the population were already Christianised. Pentecostal churches had started doing it around the same time, using guitars, drums and loud p.a. systems in some central locations in Nuku'alofa. Open-air evangelism was looked on by the traditional churches as something akin to stealing people from other denominations.

The earliest attempts originating from the Gospel Fellowship were very basic. A couple of Peace Corp volunteers, Patti and Russ Foss, teamed up with Colleen, myself, Paula Afuha'amango and 'Ofa Fatafehi. The Peace Corps is an independent agency and programme of the United States government that trains and deploys volunteers to provide international development assistance. Patti and Russ were Christians who we appreciated just for the company of other palangis.

At the first open-air, we set up under the veranda of a small store on Railway Road. I played guitar, Patti and Russ made up a harmonious quartet with Colleen and Paula. It was a small start, but a start, nonetheless. By the late 70s, open-airs had developed into a strategic part of the training of youth in public evangelism.

Starting in the mid-70s, youth would arrive at our home on a Friday afternoon for games, singing, Bible study and open-air preparation. Oh, and of course, supper.

They were taught how to share testimonies and explain verses they were learning, which helped strengthen their daily Christian life. New palangi songs were introduced gradually, along with short talks about aspects of the gospel. One song that said, "I'm a debtor, I know," was hard to pronounce and came out sounding like, "I'm a turtle, I know!"

Tongan's have much more of an oral culture, so they have plenty of natural ability in public speaking. This meant that at least 50 percent of the group had a latent ability to speak publicly with varying degrees of confidence. Developing a clear and personal understanding of the gospel, however, was going to take time.

Colleen and I were blessed with musical ability, Colleen playing keyboards and a very unusual South American instrument, the marimba. Unusual for Tonga, that is. It was a bit clumsy to erect each time, but created a lot of interest. I had a degree of proficiency on the acoustic guitar that was a perfect match with the Tongan harmonies. They were certainly not short on raw talent. This new style of gospel music was a crossover between the traditional Tongan *hiva kakala* (Tongan love songs) and traditional hymns.

'Ofa and I would select roadside sites anywhere in Nuku'alofa where there was open space for people to shelter from the sun. Often this would be under the shade of a beautiful *ovava* (banya) or mango tree. One favourite spot in Ma'ofanga was near a bakery.

Though it was illegal to trade on Sundays, this bakery was one of only two in Nukuʻalofa that had a special concession. Large groups would take a leisurely Sunday afternoon walk, sometimes for considerable distances, just to get the hot, fresh bread. It seemed a perfect time and place for the young church to preach to revolving crowds about the Bread of Life.

Oftentimes, our youth were singing and sharing with their workmates or schoolmates. This added to Jesus' call of letting our lights shine. It was quite a challenge, but strengthened our resolve to obey the command, "Be witnesses in Jerusalem, Judea and to the uttermost parts of the world." The Word was spread, as was the likeable sound of a different style of Christian music on the rather quiet Sunday afternoons

Crowds of between 50 to 100 were commonplace. Conversations with listeners were such a great learning experience for new Christians and done in a non-threatening way.

The blessings of open-air ministry were far-reaching. Some observations might clarify more deeply how the gospel took root in the Fellowship in the face of strong religious and cultural opposition. Here are some very basic observations:

- Traditional Tongan church practice seemed to be about routine and rituals rather than the core New Testament values taught by Jesus to His disciples. Our open-airs, instigated by this newly-planted church, were more about taking the message of the gospel of Jesus Christ into the highways and byways. The new generation learned to take the Good News to the city, Nukuʻalofa, neighbouring villages and further out to surrounding islands.

- Traditional Tongan church function was about a professional elite – authorised leaders – conducting the primary services and rituals of the church. Open-airs were about the participation of all who had a personal story to tell of our journey of faith in Christ. They provided an ideal training ground for those with preaching gifts and gave invaluable experience in sharing up-to-date accounts of new life in Christ. It wasn't uncommon to have baptisms preceding or following the open-air programmes, which gave a vital initiation into the role of the whole church membership to evangelise.

- The traditional Tongan church preachers were chosen by a nomination and selection process at an Annual Church Conference. In the open-air ministry, there was a weekly observation of growing leaders, along with a discussion amongst the developing leadership community about who would participate next.

- Traditional Tongan churches expected attendance at their church building and no other. This meant that no one should be seen at an open-air programme. However, since open-airs were obviously outdoors and mostly during free time, it was very easy for enquirers to observe and process this new expression of faith in God in their own private space. While the open-air work was not a significant time of harvesting souls, it was definitely a valuable time of seed-sowing of the gospel. It was also a time for the clarifying of Christian truth centred specifically around the Cross.

- Traditional Tongan churches had a very strong hierarchical structure, where members were arranged on a continuum built around things like educational achievement, business acumen, seniority, and relationship to church leaders or the nobility. Participation in open-air ministry was centred on a personal vital faith in Christ and nothing else. One of the most encouraging aspects was that virtually every able-bodied person in the congregation, from the oldest to small children, would come along to where the service would take place. Older members, while they didn't take part in the singing and testimonies, provided much encouragement for the new generation.

A group called Sowers International, under the leadership of Ken Rout, played a significant part in refining us all for open-air ministry. Tonga Gospel Fellowship was added to their international training programme, and they made annual two-week visits between 1980 and 1984, and then again in 1988. Ken showed us effective ways of presenting truth. He trained six preachers in giving testimonies and illustrating messages with a paintbrush and intriguing ladder lettering. Of course, we had to use their recommended portable platform and paintboard.

Without a doubt, the open-air ministry was a cornerstone of the growth of the new churches. Conducting open-airs at least twice a month over ten years established local church evangelism as a regular practice for each of the local churches as they became established. Almost everybody in the churches experienced the theme of "together for the gospel" in a very real way. The "go and make disciples" of Matthew 28 became a regular experience for the churches. "I will be with you" increased the confidence of us all. Inevitably we returned to the chapel and spoke about how we had experienced God's presence with us.

No greater way of teaching church growth could have been found than to take new converts into new areas with a new presentation of Christian truth. To a community shaped by strong denominationalism and nearly 100 years of church tradition centred around services inside church buildings, this approach proved to be the Spirit's means of developing maturity in disciples and establishing longevity in infant churches.

Adaptations to the open-air style evolved over the years and morphed into a wide variety of presentations for a variety of situations. There was a monthly presentation to the inmates of Huʻatolitoli State Prison. As a result, I was invited to spend time with some who were in solitary confinement awaiting the death penalty. Three prisoners were hanged in 1982 during the time we visited. God, in his mercy, gave those men an opportunity to hear the Good News to the poor and the release of (spiritual) captives as they awaited their execution.

One prisoner, upon release, came to our Easter Camp in Halaleva. There, he professed faith in Christ and was baptised, but he proved to have ulterior motives. He caused some disruption in the church, which alerted all of us to Jesus' words, "I am sending you out like sheep surrounded by wolves, so be wise as serpents and innocent as doves" (Matthew 10:16 NET). There surely was a serious lesson to be learned for the young leaders.

The Annual Agricultural Show at Teufaiva (the national sports stadium) gave us another opportunity to conduct abbreviated presentations of the gospel. We also handed out the Christian literature we had begun to accumulate from Campus Crusade for Christ, Scripture Gift Mission and printed radio sermons. Some 10,000 visitors filed through on Friday and Saturday to view the great displays of Tongan home, garden and farmware. Many great conversations took place. The exposure of Christians in a setting like this was challenging but rewarding.

All these opportunities were used of God to highlight, for the growing church, the priority that must be given to church-based evangelism. The same opportunities highlighted to the general population of churchgoers that while individual churches had a responsibility to nurture our own members, the church also had a calling to take the gospel to all the people.

A Village Crusade

Another use of the open-air services was the week-long services we held in villages outside Nukuʻalofa, and especially on the Northern Island group of Vavaʻu. One such visit took a team of 15 young people. Open-air-type programmes were supplemented by the use of a movie projector and films like *Pilgrim's Progress*.

One of the first attempts at an evangelistic outreach outside of Nukuʻalofa took place at the end of 1977. Remember, the church had only been functioning for a few years.

Hōfoa was a village some ten kilometres out of Nukuʻalofa, just off the main Hihifo Road (West). Colleen had contacted Pōhiva regarding help with the pre-school mentioned earlier. Pōhiva and her husband, Siope, were a fine evangelical couple who had spent time in New Zealand and made sincere commitments of faith through the work of Capernwray, Botany. They generously used their humble home as a base for the team for a week.

A letter we wrote to Mr Greenfield (an elder of the Nelson Gospel Assembly, our commending church) on 10th December 1977 will add authenticity to this story:

> Dear Mr Greenfield,
>
> Hot off the press comes the most encouraging news since we set foot on Tongan soil nearly four years ago.
> For quite a few months, the small congregation has been praying about having a concerted gospel effort for a full week. We had plans to go to an outer island, either ʻEua or

Ha'apai, but with other commitments, a lot of equipment to transport and most of all a lack of peace about the venture, plans changed.

We decided to go to one of the closest villages to Nuku'alofa, population around 500. I have made friends in the last five months, through Colleen's Kindergarten, with a middle-aged couple, Siope and Pōhiva, who have been saved through Capernwray. They offered us the complete use of their humble home and all the conveniences. A truly moving example of Christian love and sacrifice. They did all the cooking for a group of about 15 of us, treating Colleen and I and Joel like royalty. We left last Monday lunchtime with a team of young people all having been saved since we've been here.

We planned a full schedule for each day, which started at 6 a.m. with devotions and went through till nearly 11 p.m. some evenings. After the early morning devotions, some breakfast and then general cleaning, we had a collective group study from Joshua. Our visitation of homes began around 10 a.m. The idea was to tell the village about the afternoon programmes but also to help where we could with practical jobs. Girls did washing for some older people. I got into sanding down an old dressing table. We ate lunch around mid-day and then had a debrief on the morning. Then preparation for a Good News programme for children and an open-air programme for the evening. Two Good News programmes were held at different parts of the village, with nearly 60 at each. After those programmes, we'd set up a volleyball net and involved ourselves with a lot of the local youth. The evening meal was followed by the open-air. Approximately 100 came to each programme.

On the first night, many spoke with the team and expressed

interest in a clear gospel message. On the third night, we experienced a night of reaping. I spent over an hour with one young man, full of questions about faith. He prayed a prayer of surrender to Jesus at the end of that.

By this time, all our group were so encouraged by the positive responses. On the Thursday night, after a stirring message from one of our young men, it was like the windows of heaven opened. Many people responded to a call for commitment. As a group of us walked up the dirt road in darkness, I couldn't help but praise God after seeing so many respond to an appeal.

Back at our little Tongan house, all was strangely quiet, but as I looked inside, there were pockets of threes and fours talking through the message and the gospel appeal. I walked around these groups and found so many had put their faith in Christ.

After the final night, around 50 youth from the village crammed into the small Tongan house provided by Siope and Pohiva. Without a doubt, the biggest impact was made on the young team from Halaleva. Never had they witnessed a response like this to the gospel. We counted nearly 30 people in the village had made commitments to Christ.

We now have the great task of building them up into disciples of Christ. Many cried as we packed up to leave, pleading with us to return. I'm quite sure that if the Lord directed us to plant a church there, many would be willing to join us.

I'm sure you will join with us in praise to God for the good things He has done.

Sincerely in Him,
Graeme and Colleen.

The sequel to this exciting beginning is informative. Even though Siope and Pohiva were very encouraged and supportive of the fresh work started, leaders of the denominations began to put heavy pressure on them. The group from Halaleva visited to conduct weekly Bible Studies. Some were baptised, but the numbers attending dropped off.

This was a good reminder of the sower who went out to sow (Matthew 13). This pattern of denominational opposition showed up on many other occasions. The reason being, whenever the village Chief or town officer had his own strong denominational connections, pressure was put on him to preserve the unity of the village. Ministers were, probably rightly, very protective of their patch. A clear indication that this was not a society built around democratic values but rather around extended family and religious identity.

Siope and Pohiva were made to feel foolish and divisive, but they remained faithful Christian friends and attended many of the fellowship gatherings at Halaleva. In November of 1978, the interest in studies had dwindled to virtually zilch, so we decided to stop visiting the village. It brought a lot of disappointment, but we'd learned some valuable lessons as a small church.

Chapter 14

The Gospel Sounding to Every Island

After two years and slowly beginning to use the Tongan language in a church setting, Colleen suggested I talk with the government radio station A3Z about preaching on their programme. I've already related how this opportunity came to be. It was one of the "pressure cooker" experiences of language learning. It was March 1976 when the contract was signed with The Call of the Friendly Islands. I can still hear the beautiful sound of the ancient Tongan *fangufangu* (nose flute) as Radio Tonga began its daily transmission. Just as the nose flute was used to awaken royalty, God was about to awaken people across the islands to the Good News of the gospel. Preaching the gospel over radio was additionally God's instrument of awakening the young church to their responsibility toward the whole community.

While preparing and preaching was very challenging, we had learned from the earliest days that if God opens a door, he will surely provide the means. "Go, and I will be with you" was never more appreciated than through this ministry. Colleen played the Hammond organ in the studio. Onward Christian Soldiers was the theme song, and then I preached for 30 minutes.

Again, this Christian service from a very young church thrust us into the wider religious community and under the critique of the public. Since radio was the primary means of public communication, listeners from across the Kingdom began to write in for copies of the sermons. We received invitations to visit individuals in their homes to discuss topics and texts they had heard. One significant and very encouraging comment was made quite early in the history of the programme:

"You seem to stay with explaining the actual words of scripture without digressing into political or social controversies."

Sermon topics were almost exclusively centred around a particular text and the exposition of it. Messages were always gospel-centred. This was at a time when there was a lot of unrest amongst the commoners relating to land ownership. Another was the period of drilling for oil and the excitement of striking it rich. Maybe our lack of experience and newness to the community was an advantage. We knew God and the gospel, and that is what satisfies the hunger in man's soul, whatever his political, social or financial background.

It's not usual for locals to write letters, but an invitation was given nonetheless for those who might want a printed copy of sermons. Here's one response that came in October 1977:

Dear Brother in Christ,

We shall never tire of thanking God for the love of our Saviour.
 I haven't sufficient words to thank you for your wonderful help given over your radio programme. I have come to realise that God saves by His free grace alone. Sincere love and thanks.

I had the opportunity to visit the home of one of the nobles whose estate includes a large part of the Nuku'alofa district.[31]

Honourable Fakafanua had a piano that needed tuning. I'm not a trained piano tuner, but having a good ear, a tuning fork and ratchet, why not give it a go? When Hon. Fakafanua heard my voice, he recognised it from the radio broadcasts. He then expressed deep appreciation for them. He confessed to not being a regular church attender but said he was certainly blessed by the teaching of scripture, especially from a palangi!

In 1981, I had another opportunity to visit a senior official in the Tongan Government, the Minister of Finance, Hon. Mahe 'Ulu'uli Tupouniua. We had received a generous donation of $10,000 from Elaine and Vin Satherley from Marton Bible Church to purchase a new Toyota truck to transport growing numbers to church services. I made an impromptu visit to his offices to ask permission to import the vehicle duty-free. On arriving, his secretary informed him of my unscheduled visit. He was gracious and welcoming, which surprised me, having never met him.

"Graeme," he said, "Thank you for your visit. I have so appreciated your radio messages. They feed my soul because I'm not a church attender."

After a warm conversation, he said it was fine to leave.

"But with respect," I said, "I actually came to ask your permission to import, duty-free, a vehicle for use in the community."

"Fine," he replied. "Write me a brief explanation as to how this will benefit the whole community."

We got that done, and within a week, Cabinet had given approval. Such was the broad effect of simple gospel-centred radio programmes.

After five or so years, two of the young men had grown sufficient in their faith and developed enough confidence to start sharing in the radio ministry with me. This opportunity not only helped to teach the gospel to the general population. It was an inspiration to the growing churches and gave opportunity for local preachers to prepare sermons of a specific length, with clear outlines for keen listeners. Radio ministry continues to this day, but with the added dimension of television broadcasts.

Chapter 15

Man Overboard

While all this activity was going on, tensions continued to simmer within our small fellowship, more particularly with the older leaders. However, Christians believe God causes all things to work together for good to those called according to His purpose. This is one of those stories, an outworking of that truth.

Of the church's founding members, Fine Taue, had migrated to the United States, and the others were not showing the same spiritual interest as Tuʻulaki. Remember, Setaleki and Siaosi had questioned me in our first few months about the purpose of our mission to Tonga and concluded we weren't what they were looking for.

Siaosi was reasonably faithful to the services, and would often take impromptu opportunities to remind everyone of the old works salvation system. That was one of the hard parts of growing a church when original members had never experienced new birth.

Setaleki also didn't play a significant role in the spiritual leadership of the church but was not ashamed to call himself the church's "file"! In other words, his job was to keep a sharp edge, especially on the youth, in respect to culture and use of traditional language. He was known to attend kava drinking clubs and get stoned. He would come to church services only irregularly and sleep rather noisily in the back corner. He'd often wake up at the end of our worship and Bible teaching and proceed to give the young men a lecture about their dress, their improper use of Tongan language, or of making too much mess on the sacred property. It was done in a good spirit, but was nonetheless irritating to the youth. It must be said that he had a real sense of responsibility for the property and cared meticulously for lawns, gardens, fruit trees and *lou'akau* (pandas plant for weaving mats).

My relationship with Setaleki was challenging. I was very young, inexperienced and sometimes insensitive to the older members. He was the main instigator of this new church and maintained a strong sense of responsibility towards the members. After Tu'ulaki, his wife, had come to faith, she became a strong propagator of the ministry and shielded the church from some of Setaleki's unpredictable outbursts. After some time, however, my relationship with Setaleki took a turn for the better through an incident that shook us all.

One day, Tu'ulaki told us she had serious concerns about Setaleki's whereabouts. He'd left for Pangopango on a business trip, but after several weeks, there was no word if he had arrived safely. There was a chilling event about one week after he'd left that gave Tu'ulaki concern. The boat he sailed on from Nuku'alofa to Pangopango was the *Tokamea*. A wooden boat that subsequently proved to be unfit for purpose. Here's a report given by the media around that time:

> Tonga's worst ferry disaster was in December 1977. The *Tokamea*, with 63 people on board, disappeared while travelling from Vava'u to Niuatoputapu. All that was found was a life jacket and an empty deep freeze unit, despite extensive searches. It was reported to have had an inadequately plugged gash one metre long below the waterline and unserviceable radio equipment.[32]

As we know, Seta was on the *Tokamea*. The family tried in vain to contact Setaleki in Pangopango but without success. With news of the *Tokamea* disappearing, we began to fear the worst, along with the many families of those who had sailed. All of Tonga was in shock. Where was Seta? Was he lost along with the rest?

Suddenly, Tuʻulaki got the great news we'd all been waiting for. He was safe, still in Vavaʻu. She had spoken to him on the phone.

Out of a sense of great relief, I caught the next flight to Vavaʻu to see how he was. I was a bit fearful since we weren't on the best of terms. How would he receive me? I hitched a ride from the Lupepauʻu International Airport into Neiafu, with no clue where I might find him.

Arriving in Neiafu, I walked through the small run-down shopping centre asking if anyone had seen Setaleki. That might sound strange, but he was very well known, especially in Vavaʻu, his home island. Then I remembered he was a keen draughts player, a common game played with bottle tops or rocks, whatever works. Just by chance, I noticed a group of men down the side of a small *fale koloa* (dairy).

"Anybody seen Setaleki?" I called.

Slowly, this dishevelled-looking guy stood up and with much surprise said, "Kulemi, what are you doing here?"

We embraced.

"Why did you come?" he said.

"We heard about the *Tokamea* disappearing in the storm and thought you were on it!" I said. "We're all so relieved to hear you were safe, so I decided to come and check on you."

He took me by the hand, a sign of male affection even amongst older guys, and we strolled back into town.

"You're going to stay with me in this boarding house, and you can go back tomorrow. First job," he said, "Please give me a shave."

A first for me, shaving three weeks of growth off a rugged Tongan male's face. We found some razor blades and soap. I don't know who was most nervous! But in that time, I got closer physically and emotionally with him than I could ever get in normal circumstances. He told me the story leading up to this day:

> I left Nuku'alofa on the *Tokamea*, and on the first night, it was pretty rough between Tongatapu and Nomuka. I was sleeping on the top of the canopy. I was dreaming I got into a fight. I swung a fist at the guy I was fighting and suddenly found I had rolled overboard! It was just breaking dawn.
>
> I was trying my best to swim, but I was in a big army coat. I thought to myself, "This is it! I'm going to drown."
>
> Suddenly, I felt a heavy nylon line against my leg and realised it was the fishing line the crew were trawling behind the boat. They'd often caught some pretty big fish. I grabbed hold of the line for all I was worth.
>
> The guys on the boat quickly realised they'd hooked something, most likely a good-sized fish. So, the captain cut the engine, wound in the line and there I was, not at all what they expected. Was it Jonah? No, it was Seta. I realised just how lucky I was to have survived.
>
> We sailed on into the shelter of Pangai in Ha'apai and laid anchor. Apparently, the wooden boat had a serious leak just below the water line. The crew patched it over with many layers of tapa cloth we had on board. Their intention was to do a better job once we'd arrived in Neiafu, Vava'u. Of course, I intended to sail on to Pangopango once the boat was repaired. However, I'd swallowed so much seawater, I was feeling *toka kovi* (pretty crook), so forfeited my ticket and remained in Neiafu.

I was in awe of the providence of God in preserving Seta in such a remarkable way. He and I slept the night together in a boarding house and we talked into the small hours about life and death, heaven and hell. I had a great opportunity to talk through the gospel, trying to show him God's grace was all that was necessary for salvation. He didn't seem to get it at all but was moved and appreciative that I had taken the time to check on him. We began a completely new relationship from that day.

The endpoint of our relationship is worth telling as well. In 1989, after leaving Tonga permanently, we were living in Los Angeles. Setaleki and Tu'ulaki had migrated with their family to San Francisco in 1983. While studying at The Master Seminary in Los Angeles, we invited him down to our home for a weekend. We took him along to the Grace Community Church Sunday service. A congregation of around 5,000 blew him away. When we got back to our home in Santa Clarita, we talked again about the gospel, the way to be certain of eternal salvation.

Seta left me feeling very sad. He said, "I was the one responsible for the establishment of the Gospel Church in Halaleva back in 1974. That will be my passport into heaven."

I responded with Toplady's famous hymn, "Rock of Ages, Cleft for Me". It's one of the most popular Tongan hymns, as translated beautifully by James Moulton. These are the familiar words Setaleki had sung perhaps hundreds of times:

Ka ne lahi 'eku tangi
Ka ne u fai ha ngāue lahi
Ta'e'aonga ai pē ia
Ke huhu'i 'eku hia.
'Ikai ha'aku me'a 'e ma'u.
Piki pē ki he 'akau.

Nothing in my hand I bring
Simply to the cross I cling.

Naked, come to thee for dress.
Helpless, look to thee for grace.
Vile, I to the fountain fly
Wash me, Saviour, or I die.[33]

At that time, I felt he did not understand how totally insufficient his establishment of Gospel Fellowship was in giving him eternal salvation. That was what Jesus did in His death and resurrection! His family have assured us that he did finally trust in Christ alone for his forgiveness of sins in his final weeks on earth.

It was one of my sweetest memories to conduct three days of family devotions after Seta had passed away. And then at the formal funeral service, to preach to a very large crowd of mourners, many from the highest rank in Tongan Society, that Setaleki Afuhaʻamango was a servant of the Lord in enabling the gospel to take deep root in the Kingdom he loved.

Chapter 16

New Gospel Centres

By the early 1980s, the Halaleva church was 90 percent full in both the morning and afternoon Sunday services. It seemed right to start thinking about the possibility of planting churches in other centres on Tongatapu, as well as other islands.

Though the church in Halaleva was relatively young, barely ten years old, to plant other sister churches would give valuable lessons in the selection of qualified leaders and a great opportunity to see the proliferation of more vibrant evangelical communities into towns on Tongatapu, as well as the outer islands. Again, Colleen and I had no previous experience. We did have the examples detailed in Acts of the Apostles, so we began to share the vision with other leaders and pray together how God would lead us.

Just as Ernie Edwards warned some 30 years prior, if the evangelical church doesn't do something, Tonga will be overrun by cults:

> There's an appalling need for the gospel in Tonga... If nothing is done within ten years, it appears that the Islands will be largely Mormon.[34]

Many visits had been made to Vava'u, the next most populous island. However, after prayer and discussions with the growing leadership team, it was decided that a second congregation in Nuku'alofa was a good way to start. We could divide up the growing

Locations of church-plants:
1. Halaleva, 2. Touliki, 3. Manuka.
(Base map © WorldAtlas.com, used with permission)

leadership team, while also supporting each other. Practically speaking, we were getting a van full of participants from the Pātangata and Touliki districts. This took a good hour before and after the morning service. Then the same routine in the afternoons, following open-airs and an evening service. It made for a long day, especially for us with three young children.

The First Church-Plant in Touliki, 1983

Since there were already a good number of regular members living on the outskirts of Nukuʻalofa, the leadership team started to think seriously about how to go about establishing this new work. The young leaders were quite apprehensive, having never experienced such a plan. So, what were the factors that contributed to planting a church in Touliki?

It was surely providential that around the same time, Rowland Forman and a team of students from the GLO (Gospel Literature Outreach) training centre arrived for a three-week mission trip. The leadership decided to focus on visitation of the areas known as Touliki and Popua. Partnering the GLO students with our own youth provided excellent opportunities for training and experience for both groups. They were taught how to present the gospel as a basic Bible study. We used a Scripture Gift Mission booklet, *Four Things God Wants You to Know*, but expanded the study with diagrams drawn out on paper as we sat on the floor of homes.

We found many homes with people who were happy to let these young people share the scriptures. While the Kiwi students did the basic presentation, the Tongan partner translated and ad-libbed to keep the listeners involved in the three-way conversation. That first visit from a GLO team provided a template for door-to-door evangelism that continues to this day.

As a result, several families showed interest in ongoing Bible studies as well as visiting formal church services. A recent interview with one of the New Zealand students may give some interesting insights into the "sender/sent" relationships and the impact of GLO visits.

These are some of Joanne Shirtliff's recollections after 40 years. She can be forgiven for some of it being a bit blurry!

One song we often sang as we drove to different events and excursions in 1983 was:

> I'm gonna stay right under the blood,
> I'm gonna stay right under the blood,
> I'm gonna stay right under the blood,
> where the devil can't do me no harm.
>
> No harm, no harm, no harm,
> No harm, no harm, no harm.
> I'm gonna stay right under the blood,
> Where the devil can't do me no harm.

The best memory was the beautiful harmony of Tongan and Palangi joining together to the accompaniment of the guitar that came out as we trundled along in the back of the vehicle. And one of the boy's names was Moses.

I remember going out to the lower-income villages and the honour we were shown/given by the folk we visited. It was humbling.

I remember the beautifully laid-out feasts we went to, and the honour we were given; again humbling. I remember stepping out in culinary courage with some of the food and eating things one only tastes when learning cross-cultural lessons! Mmm. (I probably felt like saying "yuck" a few times, but I was raised well to give it a try anyway.) And well, I survived to tell the tale.

I remember the joy I encountered so often at these visits from the folk we talked with. That was moving. They made us feel very special for being there.

I remember a small pig we took in the back of the truck on an outing we were having together with a few of the Tongan guides. We were thinking how cute it was to have the piglet on board and thought it to be just a pet, only to find out it became dinner later on!

I remember the singing we enjoyed so much with the group being led by Graeme and Colleen and performing at the different events we were scheduled to share at – children's programmes, church and during the radio programming. It was a double-blessing experience. We had a lot of laughs while we practised, performed, then prayed forward into the event that we would be not only a blessing but learn much about other folks' ways of life and Christian experiences.

I remember growing in my understanding of cross-cultural missions. The learning experiences have served me greatly in these following years working and living with other cultures around the USA, a little bit of Europe, the UK and here in NZ, within education, tourism and ranger work with NZ Conservation in the backcountry.

I remember some of those cultural differences back in Tonga and other countries making me feel challenged and sometimes even sad, wishing I could change things. One thing I did come away with from my first cross-cultural experience of Tonga was, always start with prayer.

Prior to the visit of the GLO team, nature had a part to play in helping to make deeper connections with people seeking the knowledge of God for themselves rather than merely something handed down by tradition.

Can you believe God can use an apparent disaster to contribute to a church-plant?! In March of 1982, Hurricane Isacc wreaked havoc across the southern groups of Ha'apai and Tongatapu. At once, our faithful New Zealand church partners and relief organisations made contact to offer help, including $50,000 from Tearfund.

A couple on the tiny island of Kotu in Ha'apai – Mana and Ana Pepa – contacted us following one radio broadcast. Isacc had destroyed most of their means of livelihood. A coconut tree had blown directly across their boat, crushing it. Colleen and I gamely made plans to visit Kotu. Taking Janita and Joel on the interisland ferry *Olovaha* only got us to Nomuka. We then had to transfer, in the open sea, by jumping down into a small tinny (a three-metre aluminium boat with a 15-horsepower motor). Then a 35-kilometre trip in the dead of night through the surrounding reefs to their island. There was a small convoy of four boats for safety! Life jackets hadn't been heard of in Ha'apai.

Travelling over a flat sea in the black of night with the constellations as our canopy was an awesome experience. At one stage, the stutter of motors was shut down while the group listened for the breaking of waves on the reef around Kotu. That showed them where the entrance was. We were shown true island hospitality, with two beautifully cooked crayfish to eat at 6 a.m. on the beach. A premiere breakfast for seafood lovers. By visiting Ana and Mana, our family developed a friendship and established the authenticity of that family's request for help.

Through the generosity of Tearfund, five wooden crafts were designed and built along with two longboat (seven-metre) hulls purchased for those who had suffered loss in the hurricane. One was given to Mana and Ana, and the rest distributed to others who had suffered loss.

Mana and Ana began a warm friendship with the Gospel Church and, in 1983, moved to Nukuʻalofa with their family of five. They grew in their understanding of the gospel and wanted to join the church. They had friends from Haʻapai who had previously migrated to Tongatapu. These friends allowed them to build a small home in the same area we had decided to plant the new Touliki Gospel Fellowship.

Another part of the providential plan in starting the church-plant was the provision of small hexagonal dwellings with three-metre-long walls. Colleen's father had these made and sent for those whose homes had been demolished, one of which we gave to Mana and Ana. They had shown potential as leaders and became part of the team to plant the church.

So, with three families from the Halaleva church who lived in the district, interested families from the GLO Mission and Ana and Mana from Kotu, we set out to grow the next congregation.

Of course, there was a natural initial enthusiasm within these families, not only for fellowship, but the strong desire to reach out to other new residents. The group began meeting in Mana and Ana's small house. Each week they would move all their clothes into one corner. The congregation would squat tightly into the hexagonal space and pretty much gather around the remembrance table, not unlike the original Eastern meal setting.

Within a couple of months of meeting for worship, the group initiated a discussion about how to build a small independent structure to house up to 40 people and call that their "worship centre". The owners of the land, Tonga and Elisiva Lotoʻāniu, offered the mature coconut trees on their land for timber. Approximately

15 mature trees were cut down into 10-foot logs, loaded by manpower onto a truck and transported to a small mill run by the Agriculture Department in Tokamalolo. After a month, the wood was delivered. One of the congregation, Andrew (an Australian builder, with his Tongan wife, Lesieli), helped construct a very basic building in which to hold the services.

The church grew through regular Bible studies during the week and regular visitation of the surrounding families. Baptisms were held less than one kilometre away on the foreshore, just alongside Queen Salote Wharf, provided the tide was right! Things were humming along.

But the building of a proper worship centre wasn't finished yet. In 2004, after we had settled back in New Zealand, Northcross Community Church in Auckland, specifically Mr Phil Aish, made contact and asked us if we could use a 40 × 20-metre industrial building of his that needed to be deconstructed to make way for a rapidly growing North Shore residential area. Wow, what an offer! A team removed the roof and sides. The steel trusses, along with the iron, were loaded onto the deck of a ship bound for Tonga. Six months later, a team of builders from MMM (Mobile Mission Maintenance) went across and erected Touliki Gospel Church. It still thrives, with a congregation of new families with much potential for spiritual growth in the developing area.

Planting a new church in close vicinity to the original Halaleva congregation allowed for a great partnership and participation in growth. There was much interdependence as leadership teams grew to take independent responsibility for each congregation. There are obviously many gaps that could be filled in describing the growth and expansion of Touliki Fellowship. It has been a work of God, with the families dwelling together in purpose and unity.

Amsterdam International Conference of Evangelists

With lots of energy-sapping activity in the life of the mission, we were paying a high price for the sake of the gospel. With the loss of our dear Brent (1983), grieving was also taking its toll. God was not unaware of the need for some inspiration to keep going.

For some outside stimulation I received the *Moody Monthly*, which always provided great articles to keep us refreshed. In the June edition, I noticed an advertisement for evangelists to apply to the Billy Graham Organisation to attend the International Congress to be held in Amsterdam in July. It appealed to me as an opportunity for refreshment. I fired off a letter with a brief explanation of the Tonga situation, hardly expecting a response. But within two weeks, it came. While driving to Pātangata on a Sunday morning, I was waved down by a man from the Tonga Telephone and Telegraph Department. He obviously recognised the large blue gospel truck we'd fitted out for transportation.

"McNae, I have a telegram for you," he said.

I opened it and could hardly believe what I read. The Billy Graham Organisation had made airline bookings and hotel bookings to attend. Wow, what excitement. I flew to New Zealand, then Los Angeles and finally Amsterdam. 19-plus hours! It was a surprise and joy to be seated beside another representative to the conference, Dr Steve Kumar, the well-known Christian apologist. He later visited Tonga taking lectures, some of which I tried to translate. Many of you will know the vocabulary of apologetics and philosophy is advanced. Only the Lord knows if I got some of the translation right!

The experience in Amsterdam was inspirational to say the least. The opening ceremony paraded 133 representatives with flags of their countries. Since I was the only representative from Tonga, I was the honoured flagbearer. But the worship, Bible exposition and fellowship with 4,000 of God's servants from around the world felt like a foretaste of heaven. I returned to Tonga with renewed vision and passion to "declare the praises of him who called us out of darkness into his marvellous light" (1 Peter 2:9). In hindsight, how gracious and generous of the Lord to give an opportunity like this, at a time when Colleen and I were both feeling bewildered and worn-down. Hearing testimonies of other evangelists around the world meant that coming back to continue planting churches was at the top of my agenda.

The Growth of a Church in Manuka

As the church in Touliki grew and matured, along with growing lists of contacts from across Tongatapu Island, we began to look towards the eastern end of the island for possibilities of a new centre to establish a church. We regularly received letters from radio listeners. A couple of families in Muʻa, the old capital, were showing interest. We conducted Bible studies for two months but sensed that the families were not hungry for the fellowship. There were other contacts, however, who lived another 15 kilometres around the coast in Manuka. Ana and Mana's extended family, Foulata and Tinitale Taʻufoʻou, were invited to Halaleva. They began attending services, but the 50-kilometre round trip each Sunday was expensive.

Around the same time, I had another "chance meeting" with a man from Manuka who claimed to be the Town Officer. Kaluseti and I met on the foreshore of Nukuʻalofa, much like the meeting of Foster with Setaleki. He told me that he and his wife, Lilio, had listened to and appreciated the radio broadcast for some time. We were invited to their home and began weekly Bible studies with them.

Within a few months, word got around the village of the new Gospel Church coming to the village, and a small group of interested people gathered on Sunday mornings for worship and Bible teaching in Kaluseti's house. As the numbers grew Kaluseti graciously agreed to gifting us a plot of his land that we could lease through the government. That enabled us to build a small centre to seat up to 60. Things seemed to be moving along slowly, but a critical part of establishing a new church is the maturity and integrity of the resident leaders. Unfortunately, this was not the case for Kaluseti. Some serious issues were spreading through the village around his social behaviour. Sadly he and Lilio left the group. But already, others attending were keen to hear the Word of God and learn from it. Two leaders from the Halaleva congregation played a significant role in taking mid-week Bible studies. They helped to establish the congregation in basic studies of the gospel and answered many questions about the structure of this new church.

A couple of years after we left Tonga, a request was made from the Manuka church for a more permanent building. Eventually, a team of dedicated people from Ngaire Ave Chapel in Auckland got together under the leadership of Stuart Savill and Max Guptill, and constructed a more permanent, yet simple, worship centre. It is a wonderful testament to the mission orientation of New Zealand Gospel churches that so many groups sacrificed so much to help the mission's growth in Tonga.

Underlying the growth of these small churches was a sociological principle that is helpful to grasp. Tongan society, being strongly hierarchical, has an inbuilt loyalty. This loyalty is reflected throughout the extended family and down to the village and island group one is born into. By extension, this loyalty has developed to the denomination one is born into.

Without going into historical detail, most traditional denominations have had very turbulent, even acrimonious experiences.

Attempts have been made by royalty and clergy to reconcile differences without success. Then, with the influx of cults, declaring that any belief outside of their "truth" was demonic, barriers were further strengthened. This could possibly be why, when the Gospel Churches applied for registration with the government in 1973, His Majesty King Taufa'ahau said this would be the last. Some of the fragmentation of traditional denominations centred around dissension and jealousy amongst the foreign missionaries themselves. Some of it centred around allegiances to local chiefs and the political power they possessed.

More recently, the influx of parachurch organisations had, in some cases, caused significant loss of membership from the traditional churches. These groups possessed a fresh and vibrant expression of Christianity that gave tired traditional churchgoers an opportunity to gather around these values rather than the traditional church practices. For example, the Tonga Scripture Union offered a well-structured system of daily Bible readings along with stimulating comments on those readings. Small group meetings began where the focus was on what had been learned from the Word. Hunger for this fresh approach to Christian living, along with the charismatic leadership of Rev Senituli Koloi of Scripture Union, was the most outstanding example of such parachurch influence. In fact, during the time of our church-planting, a significant breakaway from the Free Wesleyan Church occurred. Around 2,000 people left, and deep feelings of distrust of parachurch groups grew within the traditional churches as a result.[35] In hindsight, this could be why we were viewed with such suspicion. This was the environment in which the planting of Gospel Churches took place, but Colleen and I were virtually oblivious to that past history.

How vital then is the teaching of the New Testament around the unity of believers in local congregations. It must be begun by the Spirit and subsequently maintained by walking in the Spirit (Ephesians 4:1-6).

North to Vava'u

By the late 1970s, God had been moving in ways far beyond expectation. Given that the Gospel Fellowship movement was a new church in Tonga – without any fanfare, high-profile Tongan leadership or denominational history – its growth seemed quite without social or economic catalysts. It really did feel like a spontaneous work of God generating changed lives, resulting from systematic, engaging Bible teaching coupled with purposeful evangelistic involvement. All these factors combined to create a great vibe for all involved. A small group ministry was developing in homes, making it easy for new people to sit in and observe. Open-airs and radio preaching seemed to be stimulating growing interest.

With the Halaleva church well established in Nuku'alofa, and a sister congregation in Touliki, there was further interest in the outer islands, especially the northernmost group of Vava'u. A song sung by the Continental Singers during their visit began to resonate in my heart:

It's time we God's people
Stood up for what is right.
It's time we squared our shoulders back,
And raised our hands to fight...

The chorus was particularly relevant:

Step into the water,
Wade out a little bit deeper,
Wet your feet in the water of His love.[36]

194 | *Fangufangu Mana*

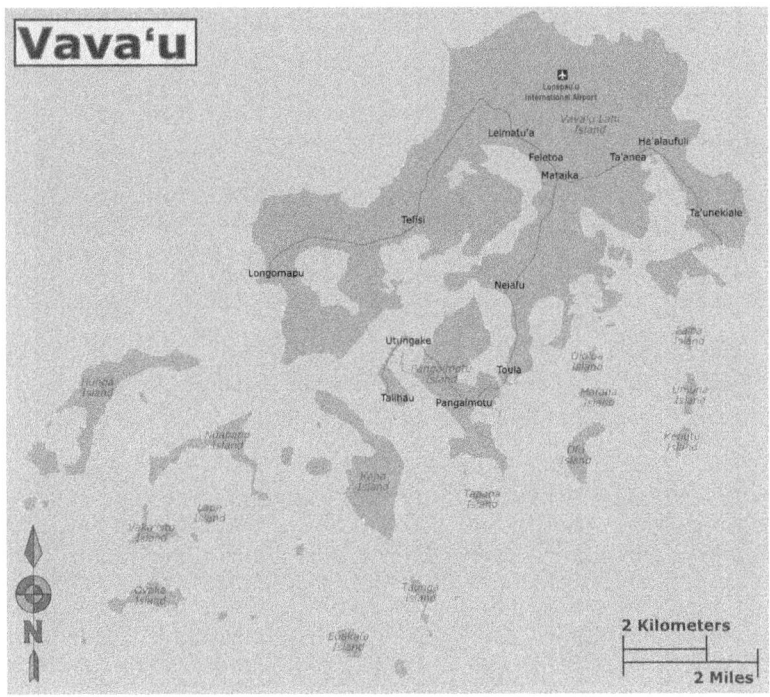

Vava'u.
(Map by Saqib Qayyum, creative commons)

Several migrants from the Northern Islands had shown interest in the Halaleva church so Vava'u began to capture our interest. Vava'u is the northernmost group, with 40 small islands. It has one of the most secure and beautiful harbours in the world, so has been the shelter for sailing vessels of all kinds for hundreds of years. It is a popular destination for yachties, the attraction being deep-sea fishing and whale-watching. The population of Vava'u was approximately 12,000 at the time, and most of the wealth of the island came from lucrative cash crops grown on very rich volcanic soil.

It was from Vava'u that the first Christian missionary left for Fiji. Sioeli Pulu was spoken of in the introduction.

I had made a sortie to Neiafu early in 1977, looking for one of the earliest contacts, a friend of Setaleki, Sosi Lopeti. I tried in vain to find him, so after three lonely nights in Neiafu decided, homesick, to return to my family. There, tied up at the wharf, was a wooden boat, about 50-foot, the *Pulupaki*. Quite spontaneously, I jumped aboard.

Well, what a trip! After just one night at sea, chugging along at about 15 knots, we suddenly cut the engine in the lee of a small island in the Ha'apai group. I was fascinated to see one of the crew dive overboard with a large spanner in his hand. Intriguing. Was I about to learn of a new fishing technique? I threw on a diving mask from my bag and jumped over to see what was going on. It was the minor matter of tightening up the very loose bolt on the bottom of the shaft that was holding the rudder on, just! OK then.

Once home, our prayer was, "Lord, how can you create an opportunity to make contact with interested people in Vava'u?" The answer was not long in coming from a very unexpected source – a clubbed-foot operation on a toddler from Leimatu'a. Does that sound like God at work? The detail follows, but first Meliame Katoa's life-change...

Manga Ono – The Six-Road Junction

One of the boasting places of the small village of Leimatu'a is the six-road junction. Actually, only three roads lead to significant destinations, the others just to small settlements of the village. Nonetheless, Leimatu'a is the first significant village next to the Lupeau'u International Airport.

How the Leimatu'a assembly came to life is one of the wonderful stories of the *fangufangu mana*, God supernaturally bringing the good news into the village. The most authentic way of relating this is to let Meliame tell it in her own words:

> I was 16 when I first heard a presentation of what I now know as the gospel through Bible Studies shared in my village by two sisters, Meleane and Tupou. They were visiting from Tongatapu, where they had become part of Campus Crusade for Christ. When they told me about Christ, I somehow knew that was what I had been waiting for. I had an emptiness in my heart, so I followed them. Sometimes, we studied the Bible three times a week.
>
> One day, Meleane asked me, "Do you want to ask Jesus to come into your life?"
>
> I didn't know how, but she led me. I'll never forget the day my soul was healed; December 1978, I accepted Christ. I felt lost when Meleane and Tupou returned to Tonga, but they encouraged me to listen to a radio broadcast by a palangi, Graeme McNae. So for about four months, I tuned in and learned so much.
>
> In April of 1979, my whole family took a trip to Tonga for the medical treatment of one of my nephews, Atunaisa. He was treated by an Australian orthopaedic specialist, Ian Stratton, who was from St Vincents Hospital in Sydney and

making regular visits to treat babies with club feet.[37] My whole family came down for the treatment and lived with my aunty and uncle, Paula and Tuna, on Hala Pili Road, less than a kilometre from the Gospel Fellowship, though we knew none of that at the time.

What happened on the first Sunday was like a miracle. My father, Kakala, was a very strict Wesleyan and had never entered another church building besides the Free Wesleyan Church. So, on this first Sunday, we all went to the Methodist Church in Halaleva.

Kakala, as usual, followed us from about 100 metres behind. It was a fine sunny day, but as he was strolling up the road, a sudden squally shower came out of nowhere. Kakala told us he looked on one side of the road for shelter, but it was just *sāfa* (long bush grass) and coconut trees. On the other side, however, he saw a building with a small patio out the front. He made a beeline for the shelter, only to find it was the front of a church! As he was shaking off the rain, a young man came and greeted him. Ofa invited him inside to join the service. The miracle was, my dad went in! Like I said, he had never entered any church other than the Wesleyan. On one occasion, when some Mormon missionaries came to talk with him at his house, he got so mad, he chased them away brandishing a bush knife.

This Sunday, the rest of my family didn't wait for Kakala, but we went on to the Wesleyan service. We returned home after it was over, but no Kakala! Where could he have gone? Had he fainted in the heat and fallen beside the road? Finally, after some anxious minutes, he showed up.

"Come into the lounge," he called. We were all eager to find out what happened. We weren't allowed to eat until he told us this story.

"I went into that small church called Kōsipeli (Gospel)," he said, "and heard an amazing message, the best talk I've heard in a long time."

Our whole family was stunned. Dad talking positively about a different church than the Wesleyan! Then he said something even more outrageous.

"I was invited to their evangelistic message at 4 p.m., and we're all going."

So, we all went (of course) to Halaleva Gospel that afternoon. The preaching was outside, and a small group of young people were singing. I remember watching a lovely girl, Alilia, and feeling something very new was happening to our family. We were invited after the service for a cup of tea and Tongan *keke*, delicious, deep-fried buns. We were deeply impressed with how our family was welcomed and loved, the first time we had experienced anything like it.

Following that life-changing day, Graeme and others from the church visited us many times a week. We quickly became family. Graeme would bring over a small hand-driven tape player with recordings of the testimonies of the youth. Our whole family would listen as these stories were told and so began the journey to know Christ personally. Something we had never experienced.

In 1980, my family decided I should move to Tongatapu for schooling. It was then my spiritual life began to grow. I joined all the church Bible Studies and started the TEE course (Theological Education by Extension) from Christian Leaders' Training College, Papua New Guinea. Sunday morning preaching fed me deep truths I had never learned before. I also became part of the visitation team that took booklets across the whole of Tongatapu. I had many conversations with all types of people. This was how my faith grew.

Now the Halaleva church family had developed a strong relationship with Kakala and Tonga's family. Colleen and I had stuck with the family while their infant went through the operation and three weeks of recovery. It seemed like doors were opening to make a much more purposeful visit to Vavaʻu.

To this day, I can still remember Kakala saying to me, "If you would like to come to my village, Leimatuʻa, I'll make sure there is a bed for you."

He certainly did that and so much more.

In the May school holidays of 1979, a team of youth from the Halaleva church set sail on the *Olovaha* government inter-island ferry to Neiafu, Vavaʻu. I'd loaded the little Suzuki 90 motorbike on board to give some form of transport for essentials on an island that, at the time, consisted of riding on the back of some rundown truck or on horseback.

Upon arrival at Nciafu Wharf, we all disembarked, along with the motorbike. I was about to ride off when one of the women police officers came alongside and asked, "Where are you going on that?"

To which I replied, "Leimatuʻa."

"Have you got consent from the Transport Department to ride this in Vavaʻu?" she asked.

"Oh, I didn't know that was required," I said.

"Well, you'd better accompany me to the station and speak with the Chief Inspector."

That was embarrassing, especially with my team of trainee disciples watching on. Not a good start to the mission.

On the way up to the station, the officer asked, "What are you going to do in Vavaʻu?"

I explained we were from Tonga Gospel Fellowship and had come on an evangelistic trip. She asked where we were going to be based, and I told her Leimatuʻa.

Then, my heart skipped a beat when she said, "Would you like to come to my village?"

"Absolutely," I said, "but there are 15 of us."

"Not a problem," she said. "I've got family in our village, Haʻakio, and we would love to look after you."

So began a wonderful friendship with Katalina Halaifonua and her family. Once we'd got the police requirements for the motorbike sorted, the team boarded a truck taking us to the centre of Leimatuʻa, where Kakala and Tonga's home was located. There were numerous houses, all within 15 or 20 metres of each other. No fences, footpaths or street lights! Kakala and Tonga's was two rooms, one door, three push-out windows, to sleep nine children. The dimensions were approximately four by three metres. Behind the house was a slightly larger thatched construction which was the kitchen.

Kakala had arranged to have a large tarpaulin erected, held up with six strong poles cut from the bush. Such was the incredible hospitality to host us for a week. Even more courageous was his willingness to host a church group unknown to the rest of the village and without consultation with the noble of the village, Hon. Fotu. There would be repercussions to speak about later.

Part of our equipment was a portable generator and movie projector with three or four full-length Christian movies, including *Pilgrim's Progress*. We scouted around for a suitable place to show the movies, and eventually settled on Sini's tractor shed, which doubled as sleeping quarters for his herd of about 15 pigs.

Word quickly spread around the village that there would be a church group singing and a movie. Over 100 people came into the shed with mats and settled themselves for the show. The memories of the first night are still vivid to this day. A movie, especially a Christian one, would have been the main interest, along with hearing a palangi speaking the local language. We had a very basic sound system. The microphone stand was a branch from a coconut palm inside a 44-gallon drum. It worked! But about five minutes into the talk, I felt something crawling on my legs. Looking down, it was as if I was Father Christmas for the flea colony! Here I was, standing smack in the middle of the pigs' sleeping quarters. It was a momentary distraction, but I quickly got back on track to preach the Word. The fact that the shed was full of people for three consecutive nights was a sign, at least, that there was interest and entertainment in the presentation. A small group of Gospel Fellowship people was present in the village for the first time. God be praised for leading us this far.

Going back to the police officer who apprehended me on the wharf, Katalina was so keen for us to visit her village that we relocated for three nights from Leimatuʻa to Haʻakio, around eight kilometres away. There was a village hall immediately opposite Katalina's house, which was very convenient to repeat the same programmes we had presented in Leimatuʻa. Again, the hall was packed, and again, there were great opportunities for the young group to sing, give testimony and present the gospel to these interested listeners. Thankfully, this hall was used mostly for kava drinking, not a sleep-out for the local swine community.

Haʻakio is part of a trio of villages, including Houma and Mangia, all within a two-mile radius. This gave the team great scope to visit homes during the day to invite people to the night programme and share Christian tracts.

One of the most memorable occasions was knocking on the open door of a very dilapidated house in the middle of Houma. Looking up from the concrete floor was the beaming face of a shrivelled woman, Kalesita. When she heard my voice, she said, "Aren't you the preacher on the radio programme? Praise the Lord, I've been praying for years to meet you." With tears, she invited 'Ofa and me into the house. She explained that she had been ravaged by polio from a young age and lost the use of her lower body. She crabbed herself around on her arms. But her spirit was alive and well since she had previously come to know and love Jesus Christ through the Scripture Union under the leadership of Senituli Koloi.

Kalesita lived with her ageing parents. Her home became a Bethany to us, one of our God-centred places to stay during visits to Vava'u. We left her with a hand-generating tape player provided by the Christian Recording Centre, Christchurch. (Alan Packer had recorded testimonies and messages for people to listen to and ponder in their own time.) This gave the Gospel Fellowship a warm and purposeful connection with someone with great limitations but a great faith. She was excited to be able to sit and listen to testimonies and eventually meet with Christians who she had listened to on the radio.

This was the first of numerous visits made to this circuit – Leimatu'a, Ha'akio, Houma and Felemea.

On one such visit, 'Ofa and I decided to visit some villages further out on the west coast, so we walked around to the small island of Koloa. By mid-afternoon, it was time to return to Houma, where we would stay with Kalesita. The tide was very low, and so we took the shortcut across the tidal flats. Houma was barely two kilometres away, and it was very easy walking until we came to a channel right in the centre. We concluded the only thing was to get a bit wet and swim across the 20-metre gap. We were quite deceived by the strength of the current, and it seemed we were making very little progress. I had a backpack, but most significantly, my Bible. Swimming with one arm and holding a Bible above your head isn't a good way to cross a strong current. We struggled for a good five minutes, and there was some panic. Getting to the other bank was a great relief, but the Bible had been under a few times.

Finally arriving at Kalesita's place, she asked how we got so wet. "Funny," she said. "About half an hour ago, I felt concerned for you, so I stopped my weaving and prayed for you."

I still use the same Bible that bears the marks of this dunking. We became such close friends with Kalesita. We invited her to Nuku'alofa to live with us for a couple of months. Having such major mobility issues was a challenge, so we arranged for her to fly down. One can only imagine the feelings of uncertainty she experienced, but such was her faith in God she stayed perfectly trusting and always with an endearing smile. Kalesita was one of God's angels we entertained. Even with her significant limitations, she was a wonderful help around the house and cared for our children with such tenderness.

Kalesita was with us one night when a random whirlwind swept over us and folded the whole kitchen roof over onto the main house! The noise was thunderous and shocked us out of our sleep.

Kalsita said, "God will care for us, let's just praise Him."

Opposition

It would be easy to only highlight the progress of growth in Leimatu'a. In fact, the families experienced many bitter trials. From the noble responsible for the village, through to the leaders of traditional denominations and right into the core of their families, people were slandered, chased from their homes and ostracised at every turn.

Fauiki, Meliame's sister, was fearless in her witness to the treasure of knowing Christ and pointing out the emptiness of traditional religion. One day on a bus, she was sharing with a lady about the joys of the Bible studies the Gospel ladies were having.

One eavesdropper overheard the conversation and said loudly, "Don't talk to dogs like Fauiki."

Fauiki was unfazed, reminding her that even Jesus Christ was mocked by religious people. Fauiki continued to speak boldly about her faith in Christ to the whole bus, testament to her boldness for Christ!

The *eiki* (village noble) voiced his displeasure as well. Hon. Fotu had two older boys. They relocated to Tongatapu for education, and their home faced the rear of the church property in Halaleva. Our young men befriended 'Ului and Fatani, and after a short time, they joined in with studies, open-airs and prison visits. News reached their father, who was not happy. After Ului professed faith in Christ and was baptised, it was too much for the Hon. Fotu. He wrote a letter to Naisa, one of the new church leaders, forbidding him to have any more to do with his family.[38]

As an interesting sequel to this issue, John Komene visited Tonga in August 1986. John and I decided it might be diplomatic for a Māori leader of his reputation to meet Fotu personally. I introduced John to Fotu using appropriate Tongan language. John then greeted Fotu with a mihi whakatau. John had his formal rakau korero (talking stick) and with his usual authority and passion, introduced himself. This was significant, as he was showing honour and respect. Fotu was moved and humbled by John's mihi. He proceeded to wish us well in the preaching John had come to do. This engagement seemed to diffuse some of the ill-feeling between the village chief and this fledgling congregation.

Continued Growth for Leimatu'a Church

That first trip to Leimatu'a in 1980 set in motion a new set of relationships with Kakala and his extended family. Though it put the whole family in line for criticism from the Wesleyan church leaders and the town noble, even more difficult was the reaction of Kakala's wife, Tonga. She was a zealous participant in the women's programme "The Angels". They were particularly devout in their early morning weekly prayer and fasting regimes. Kakala's adult children came under increasing animosity from their mother, one of the daughters being chased from the family home.

But God was at work in individual hearts. Fauiki was one of Kakala's four daughters, married to Pila Tāpui. I would sleep in Kakala and Tonga's small two-room house. I had the bedroom, while the rest of the family of 10 slept in the other room. Pila and Fauiki were so keen to learn that I would have a one-hour Bible study with them at least three days a week. Pila was a dedicated gardener with about ten acres of cash crops. He had taught himself to read and write after finishing school. Their zeal to learn gospel truth was inspirational. They had close family and friends in Ongo and Nanise, Sione, Naomi and Tina, whom they evangelised. Within the year, they would join the studies in Pila and Fauiki's *fale Tonga* (thatched house).

Another couple, Tupou and Filipine, who were close neighbours of Fauiki, made their own independent contact with the Gospel Fellowship after listening to a radio sermon.

The text was John 14:6, with the common greeting, "Where are you going?" (*Ko ho'o 'alu ki fē?*)

Tupou asked for a visit the next time I was in Leimatu'a. Both he and his wife came to personal faith in Christ and joined the growing group of new Christians.

In the meantime, two of Kakala and Tonga's daughters had moved to Tongatapu. Meliame, to attend high school at Lavengamālie, a new church school set up by the Tokaikolo Fellowship. Fifita came down to live with us and help look after our children during Colleen's busy activities.

After two years of visits to Leimatu'a (1985-1986), the group had grown to five families. By the mid-80s, a strong bond had developed with a growing number of believers there. The family of Kakala had moved to Tongatapu for education. They had been baptised and become an integral part of the disciple-making structure of the church. The families in the new fellowship were nearly all cash-crop farmers. Greatest of all, the criticism this group experienced helped to refine their understanding of the sufficiency of Jesus Christ's death for salvation. This contrasted with the old belief that our good works had merit to save us. It united us together with them into a new spiritual family.

The time had come for the leadership of the Halaleva church and the leaders of the Leimatu'a group to decide to build their own worship centre. That would mean the appointment of leaders in the Leimatu'a church.

In August 1986, a small building was erected on land belonging to Viliami Tāpui. Without any fanfare or great feasting, the Gospel Fellowship of Leimatu'a was opened and the essential services of communion, Bible teaching, prayer and fellowship began. The spirit of evangelism had begun virtually from the time each of the members had experienced their new birth in Christ.

Those who made up the congregation included Pila mo Fauiki Tāpui, Ongolea, Ongo mo Nanisē Ongolea, Fetokai, Sione mo Naomi Ongolea and Tina and Manu. Some 20 years later, a new plot of land was registered with the Tongan Government. The Deed of Lease was for 20 years and signed until May 15th, 2012. A large warehouse was given from Tauranga, New Zealand, and was erected by New Zealand volunteers and a much larger congregation.

Chapter 17

The Senders and the Sent[39]

A critical part of cross-cultural mission, such as that between New Zealand and Tonga, requires the responsibility of both the sending body and the missionaries sent. The most important reason is foundationally modelled in the scripture itself. There, the sender is Jesus Christ, as described in Matthew 28, he himself being a "sent one". Jesus made a concise statement in John 20 that can't be unpacked in such a short book as this. But the words, "As the Father has sent me, so sent I you," have intrinsic power. As the mission spread out from Jerusalem under the leadership of the twelve apostles, we have plenty of examples of the responsibilities of the missionaries to the local Christian communities of Jerusalem and Antioch. These responsibilities began with church congregations selecting and approving missionaries, followed by the missionaries reporting back with the results of their gospel preaching. Responsibility was also demonstrated by discussions to clarify issues relating to culture and Jesus' teaching (Acts 15), as well as reciprocal support for social needs, e.g. the famine in Jerusalem and spiritual support to preserve gospel purity (e.g. the issues in Galatia and Corinth).

In the case of a young couple with little formal training being sent to a country without other representatives of the Gospel Movement, other forms of affirmation were required.

Foster Crane was part of Fiji Gospel Churches with a team of Christian missionaries from Gospel Assemblies in New Zealand.

His affirmation of our suitability to the Tonga mission, along with the local churches' commendation, would have been part of the matrix of responsibility from the sending churches.

Prior to the recent documenting of sending church responsibilities,[40] the primary responsibility rested with the local church of the prospective missionary. This gave the local eldership (usually a minimum of three godly men) the opportunity to assess the spiritual maturity and suitability of missionary candidates. The initiative to want to serve in Christian mission came from the individual Christians. It was then the responsibility of the elders and congregation to hear a description of the call. If they affirmed that the call was indeed genuine, the local church would make a statement of commendation. Many times, congregations to whom the prospective missionary belonged would offer a joint commendation.

In the case of Colleen and I, commendation was given by Nelson's Rutherford St Assembly and Fenton Park Bible Chapel. An example of such is included in the appendices.

The outworking of the responsibility of the sending churches was firstly established through three dedicated men – Foster Crane, Dr Clyde Vautier and Dr Victor Wilson. Prior to us relocating to Tonga, these three men had established a Tonga Gospel Fellowship trust with three Tongan leaders, which gave us an umbrella of support through regular communication as well as annual general meetings.

However, we experienced an even more significant partnership with Dr Vautier. As mentioned earlier, he played a critical role in both the spiritual oversight and administrative structure for the development of the churches in Tonga. This was outworked consistently over a period of ten years through his mentoring by mail and his personal and often intense visits.

Just as the Apostle Paul was used greatly in the role of discipling new churches through visits and writing letters, so Dr Vautier, along with Mr Peter Greenfield from Nelson, wrote purposefully and powerfully. Their letters were primarily focused on our support and counsel as we learned to serve God in a very challenging environment.

One of the memorable lessons passed on by Peter centred on the issue of women wearing a head covering in church gatherings. Without getting into the various interpretations of 1 Corinthians 14, Peter's comment was, "People are more important than principles."

While this comment may seem cliché and not backed up by exposition, it did raise the important principle of negotiable versus non-negotiable, and essential versus non-essential, doctrine. From his encouragement, it was decided by the leadership that an item of clothing required for women should not be a stumbling block to their inclusion in the life of the Body of Christ. Acknowledgement of the headship of God over Christ and Christ over the Church would be critical to all believers in the fellowship. It was a great principle that guided the growing churches away from what may have become a legalistic practice. Some Tongan Churches have a constitutional rule that women must wear a covering of some sort. Any act of defiance of this rule would be disciplined by removing her covering altogether. Thankfully, Peter's comments helped to avoid that unbiblical practice.

Dr Vautier's letters of instruction and encouragement began almost immediately after the church-planting commenced. The first was in September 1974, while his last was March 1979, with over 40 letters in between. Such was his commitment that nearly all were written on both sides of an aerogramme with a typewriter! Some readers will never have heard of an aerogramme. The fact that I've kept all these letters shows the value placed on them in our mentoring relationship. I arranged a list of topics and scriptural observations passed on over the years as an illustration of the detail and depth of his support. The summary below has been taken from his letters:

Take care of individual Christians

The Apostle Paul worked with many people and recorded his prayers for many people. Part of the solid work God performed in the Tongan Gospel Churches was the result of Dr Vautier, and hundreds of others, praying out of a deep understanding of the churches and personal care for them. Some of the advice Dr Vautier gave us follows:

Take care of 'Ofa. He's valuable, guard him carefully.

Show patience with Saia, Fatulisi, Paula, Setaleki and Tu'ulaki.

Give thanks continually for God's provision of co-workers – Nigel and Melenaite Losena.

Don't get discouraged

Dr Vautier wrote to us regarding discouragement; for example, when members left for New Zealand and the USA. One comment briefly said, "Tell E to read Colossians 4:17 and do it." Obviously a response to some things shared with him about E's spiritual maturity. And again, "In regards to another key person, tell he to cast her wood into the waters of mara" over some bitterness she was enduring.

When there was significant discouragement, after what looked like a breakthrough in gospel outreach collapsed and outreach was terminated, he reminded us of examples in scripture where Paul was knocked down but not knocked out (Philippians 4:4-9; 2 Corinthians 4:9).

Engage boldly and prayerfully with challenges

Again, the mention of complex issues within the church and the country was in virtually every letter. How to negotiate the tension between senior members of the church and us, especially regarding ownership and use of property and vehicles provided by supporting churches. The vehicle provided for transport was often a contentious issue. He guided us through many problems surrounding our accommodation – we moved into five different houses in ten years. He encouraged us with Ephesians 6:1, reminding us that prayer is our main offensive weapon against spiritual attacks.

Constant reference to scriptural principles

Perhaps his most significant input came through his constant, careful and wise use of scripture. Almost every letter had references to principles that could be applied. These were more than passing references for us to study in our spare time. Rather, he often shared the meaning of Greek phrases, as in Romans 3:21-24. This was the foundation for believing in the sufficiency of the blood of Christ for salvation in contrast to the insistence of traditional churches that good works were man's part in securing salvation.

Writing even with serious health issues

One of the most moving letters came after he had been in hospital for significant surgery to remove cancer. After being unconscious some weeks, a letter to us was one of only two he wrote while recovering in hospital. He spoke of God's mercy in sparing his life, having been in darkness like Abraham. His actual words from his bed were, "Thinking much about Tonga and asking God to enlarge His garden."

What an inspiration this man was to us!

Administrative expertise
Another of Dr Vautier's great contributions to the growth of the Gospel Churches was in the field of administration. He spent hours drafting a constitution for the Tonga Gospel Fellowship Trust, and then sought confirmation from us. He insisted on a Tongan translation for the local members. Since the original document was prepared rather quickly, with only Dr Wilson, Foster Crane and the three original Tongan leaders having input, it was decided to prepare more substantial documentation with greater input from trust members. This document included a more detailed statement of doctrine, including the spiritual purposes of the charitable trust. A copy of these documents has been included in the appendices (TGF Constitution).

These documents were edited by New Zealand legal consultants and thereby provided a reliable structure for the next generation of leaders to model. Once the Constitution was completed, it was translated and presented to the congregation. Again, this was invaluable as a guide for the church to use scripture as our solitary guide for faith and practice.[41]

It is appropriate to acknowledge here the sacrifice made by Dr Vautier's wife, Kath and their family for the years of his intense commitment to this mission. Even more poignant is that he expended his great intellect, energy and passion at a time when his years had caught up with him. It is proper that we could say with him, as Paul said, "For me to live is Christ, and to die is gain." And, "Well done good and faithful servant."

The Influence of Visitors to the Mission

One of the helpful resources for this story has come through our personal visitors' book. Given as a 21St gift, it accompanied us to all the houses in which we resided. Part of the routine of visiting our home was, "Please sign the book before you leave."

Statistics of Visitors 1974-1987

Immediate family	28
For specific missions: Gospel Literature Outreach (5 visits), Sowers International (3 visits), YWAM-Logos and Anastasis, Fellow Workers Singers, Continental Singers, Bible Society, Wycliffe Translators, Easter Camp	148
Overseas tourists	122
Gospel Fellowship congregation	85
Palangi friends	104

It would be impossible to measure the influence such a wide variety of people had on the mission. Our children were nurtured and cared for by so many of the church families and endeared the youth to our children. Church services were an extension of our family life. Our children watched open-airs and participated in church services. Older girls from Vava'u and Ha'apai stayed with our family for long periods during school holidays. Joel, Janita and Gene still remember them fondly. Teuila was our first home helper, staying with us in the house in Kāpetā, Nuku'alofa. Not only did she help with the children but she was a daily teacher for us as we learned conversational Tongan. Fifita Kātoa came down from Vava'u and stayed for over a year in the house in Ananā, and provided wonderful support for Colleen as she kept up a busy schedule of ladies' meetings for the churches as well as Bible in Schools and kindergarten.

The youth of the church spent at least one night a week over many years preparing songs and testimonies for the open-air ministry. At the same time, they observed European training practices along with the interaction between husband and wife. Many of our church families have spoken of the impact of their observations on how they wanted to train their children. The routines of having a family meal together, preparing the children for sleeping, even the style of reading Bible stories and prayer as a family. They would comment on how much more participation there was with our children compared with their family prayers. A lot of personal evangelism took place inside our home. Unexpected visitors were free to ask their personal questions about faith, giving us many opportunities to show them the way of salvation. Our children watched and listened to many of those discussions.

The first mission teams to visit The Gospel Fellowship (TGF) were the singing groups Fellow Workers and Continental Singers. Both groups used TGF as their base for accommodation, transport, communication and public performances. Both were highly appreciated by the Tongan community and, because they were interdenominational, the public found it much easier to attend presentations. One presentation of particular significance was held in Fāonelua Gardens, a popular outdoor tourist venue. There were around 500 at the event. It was not effective for the reaping of new commitments to Christ but provided good Christian music and a gospel presentation. One of the greatest impacts from the musical groups was the inspiration gained for local talent to take versions of the visitors' songs and remake them with local style and harmonies. TGF, through the talent of Esafe Tokai and others, developed excellent groups and choirs that have become a significant part of TGF culture. These groups are still used in a variety of ministries, including evangelistic outreach, funerals and Easter camp events. This is a direct consequence of exposure to overseas visiting groups.

Visits from Gospel Literature Outreach (GLO) provided excellent opportunities to develop discipleship evangelism. As has often been said, this being a work without a previous history gave us the freedom to work out with new Christians and new visiting groups just how to go about the mission.

Five New Zealand teams visited Tonga in May 1979, September 1981, October 1982, August 1984 and September 1986. Students were supported by their own local churches and went through thorough preparation before each visit. This included a solid overview of the message of the Bible, essentials of the gospel, evangelism, mission and culture.

The exciting story of the GLO training centre in New Zealand was expertly documented in a book by David Burt.[42] The inspiration behind this training centre was that of a visionary, Colin Tilsley. Interestingly, he was born to gospel missionaries in the Godavari District in South India. He had conceived of new methods of evangelism using teams and literature. People and resources were provided out of a passion for the gospel. Having started the movement in Australia, he visited New Zealand and quickly found people with the same enthusiasm. In God's providence, Colin was travelling through New Zealand in 1969, promoting this vision, when he preached at Hope Gospel Hall, Nelson. I was present at a Sunday night mission address. When Colin gave a call for young men and women to commit to mission, I rose to my feet – in the very back row, mind you, and very shy of making such a stand. So, it was Colin Tilsley of GLO who fanned my mission flame before teams eventually visited Tonga.

The arrival of GLO teams was a great boost. Rowand Forman, with his teaching skills, worked together with us in developing a version of the familiar *Bridge to God* booklet. Interaction between young Tongan Christians and enthusiastic Kiwi Christians as they prepared for village evangelism was exciting. The mutual spiritual growth between both groups could only be described as a work of the Spirit. Teams of two or three, including one or two palangis and one Tongan, were nonthreatening to the homes we visited. Every day, after two or more hours of visitation, teams returned with inspiring stories of how God had helped them. There were many people who requested further visits, some attended church services, and some were baptised as a profession of their commitment to Christ.

Most of the visiting teams were accompanied by competent Bible teachers or evangelists, so a new dynamic came into play in the church services. Preachers with different perspectives from the normal Tongan-based presentations were listened to eagerly. Those who were responsible for translation were challenged to understand properly and then interpret into Tongan thinking patterns. Not always successfully! When a preacher tells a joke that isn't funny to the national hearer, it's really disconcerting for the preacher. But when the translator makes a humorous translation and the congregation laughs, the preacher is even more confused. Despite the external confusion, God's Spirit was never stymied and continued to do His work in hearts.

The stories of partnerships that developed between Christians from New Zealand churches and Tongan churches will only really be told in eternity. But for young Tongans, previously limited to their own spiritual experience, this combination of serving God with other nationalities was a wonderful catalyst for their spiritual maturity.

On a practical level, the hospitality shown these teams by the

Christian families was generous beyond description. 2 Corinthians 8 reminds us of Macedonian Christians giving joyously out of poverty. While there was no expectation laid upon the national Christians, their generosity spoke volumes of the sincerity of faith. Never was there a word from any family relating to the burdens laid upon the church because of these visits.

Having GLO teams come at this stage of the growth of the church was providential for both the mission in Tonga and the supporting churches of New Zealand. Leadership in Tonga was very much in its formative stage, so to begin with there were no dogmas. These can grow over decades and provide stumbling blocks during the processes of working together cross-culturally. Local leadership had no specific expectations about how to serve, since they were experiencing this relationship for the first time. This seemed to be a perfect opportunity for local maturing leaders to crystallise the essence of gospel-based mission, sharing the fundamentals of a relationship with Christ, while at the same time being alert to the social and physical needs of the people who were visited.

Many times, the culture shock experienced by GLO teams during visits to places like Pātangata, one of Tongan's poorest areas, was palpable. The conversations they had with their Tongan counterparts during the visiting raised important issues for those of both sides of the cultural divide. Both were able to recognise that Jesus came to make men spiritually rich rather than economically comfortable. There was certainly no room for the so-called prosperity gospel in these situations.

There were some occasions when relationships between GLO students were quite inappropriate in the mission setting. Conversations around the correction of such behaviour involved the developing local leaders. This was particularly helpful in keeping both cultural groups focused on what is honouring to the Lord and what helps to make the gospel attractive to somewhat strict and legalistic observers.

Since Colleen and I were ourselves experiencing a steep learning curve in growing churches within a totally foreign culture, GLO leadership provided necessary and extremely helpful counsel. It was Rowland Forman who made the bold challenge that we should appoint elders for the church in Halaleva, even though they may not have attained maturity. One of the most significant outcomes of partnership with GLO was the participation of six of the developing leaders in the Shepherds' Conference at Totara Springs.

Shepherds' Conference 1987

Gene Gibson, from Fairhaven Bible Chapel in Oakland, California, had visited New Zealand for the first Shepherds' Conference at the GLO Training Centre in Te Awamutu. With the success of that visit, another was conducted, this time at Totara Springs, Matamata. Mr William McDonald, an itinerant Bible teacher, and Mr Mark Porter headed up a much larger conference. New Zealand churches and trusts provided funding for the visit. Included in the visit were those taking a leading role in the growing churches from Tonga, Naisa Ngalu, 'Ofa Fatafehi, Tali Vakalahi, Hema Pa'ila, Esafe Tokai and Fine Ngalu.

The concentrated studies gave this team an opportunity to collectively process some of the biblical principles relating to the various giftings of leaders within the local church. As a result, they gained a much-needed vision for restructuring in Tonga. To have a team travel together, study together and wrestle together with the principles has had long-lasting benefits. Local leaders were able to better identify individual giftings and discuss a way forward on their return. Structures were set up within the wider leadership for administration, evangelism, discipleship and pastoral care.

This seemed to be God's providence in preparing the churches for our departure. Such systems had not been part of the traditions of other church movements in Tonga. Most had been built around constitutions that had been drawn up decades earlier, with many denominational systems degenerating into legalism, nepotism or church splits.

Visits from Bible Teachers

Besides the mission groups, visiting speakers made their own unique contributions toward the maturing and consolidation of God's work. How some of these came to make their visits is a mystery, but they were all used greatly by God.

Agnes and Jim Boswell visited from Ontario, Canada, for two weeks in 1978. Jim had an extensive ministry with Voices for Christ in Canada. He was a passionate preacher and a lover of great hymns. I was in the early stages of using the Tongan language, and since he was such a fluent and powerful preacher, my job as interpreter was really put to the test. He taught us a very memorable chorus from his preaching in 1 Peter: "It matters to him about you." As one of the earliest preachers to visit, he left a lasting impression on the young congregation.

Maika Bovoro, a representative for the Bible Society of South Pacific, visited in March 1978. His fatherly manner and deep commitment to the scriptures was a wonderful introduction of a Pacific Island leader to the Gospel Fellowship. Maika was also a leader in the Gospel Churches in Fiji, so this immediately gave the growing churches confidence that this new movement had roots not only in the Pacific but also worldwide.

Many other preachers and teachers visited from Fiji, offering their own expression of Christianity. These included Geoff Harland, missionary to Fiji, and Francis and Nancy Byrne. Francis and Nancy were managers of Burns Philip, Tonga, and so resided in Tonga for a couple of years. Francis' gospel preaching in English helped several educated Tongans find faith in Christ. Penaia Samusamuvodre and his wife were also resident in Tonga and contributed significantly to the local assembly. Joe Samy from CEF Fiji came too. Brian Stokes taught at the 1980 Easter camp and humorously reminded everyone how banana plantations can provide lessons for Christian living.

Kanda and Fatima Sami came to Tonga in 1987. Kanda worked as an aeromechanic for the local airline. He and Fatima established deep friendships with many of the congregation. He was a very competent Bible teacher, speaking at many official occasions in the church calendar. They remained in Tonga for several years after we left and have returned for several visits. Kanda has contributed significantly to the ongoing encouragement and support of the church up until today.

Steve Kumar made several visits, coming as one of the first Christian apologists to the Kingdom of Tonga. He was quickly contacted by a local Bible college, Faith Seminary, and contributed to the learning of their students. His depth of knowledge and presentation of the reliability of Christian truth was greatly appreciated by the more educated population. While Steve was a wonderful supporter of Christian truth, the greater challenge was to those who had to interpret the new range of terms associated with apologetics. Only God knows what Tongans understood through the faltering translations. Many times, I had no idea how to explain the philosophical concepts.

Robert Early and Kemp Pallesen visited as representatives of Wycliffe Bible Translators. They conducted courses on translation at the University of South Pacific. Both made a great impression on the local church. They had a depth of experience among many

Polynesian cultures that was extremely helpful to missionaries and church members.

This is but a short list of the preachers and teachers the Lord led to inspire the growth of the fellowship. Ces Hilton, Ross Conwell and Brian Goodwin were among others who came to Tonga with the Word of God burning in their hearts and returned with the testimonies of new believers who had been delivered from stagnant Christianity.

The influence of these visits from across the world and the spectrum of para-church organisations has been profound. In a small country, independent from the larger world and most especially divided by denominationalism, a new fellowship was given a glimpse of the diversity of the Body of Christ. Co-operation within the Body of Christ was provided, even if only in short bursts of activity. To function together as fellow members of the universal Church, not simply as the local church, even for just a few weeks, provided excellent opportunities for deeper reflection and growth.

From the local hosts' perspective, these visits were often draining, even exhausting. However, interaction gave new Christian households opportunities to serve and learn truth together with the visitors they were hosting.

Foster Crane, who had a powerful fathering influence in the Pacific Islands, used to say that once a believer from the Islands had left for a more affluent lifestyle, relocating to Australia, New Zealand, the USA or the like, it was rare that they would return and contribute to their country of origin. The church today in Tonga is led and trained by those who have learned in the school of experience over the past 50 years. The visits of the Lord's people from across the world have made a significant contribution to the faithfulness of the men and women who have remained steadfast to the glory of God in their own land.

Family

Maintaining regular contact with our immediate families played a strong part in our mental and social wellbeing. To have our parents, siblings and members from our church families visit was extremely reassuring. Twenty-eight visits over the 15 years from our home churches and family members meant there were always people praying and who could be called on for a variety of needs. Welcoming these guests into the churches and, in many cases, our church members' homes, was of great mutual benefit. Our Tongan families once again showed their great hospitality, which always left a deep impression.

I vividly remember taking my mum and dad to the Fatafehi family in Pātangata, one of the poorest parts of Nukuʻalofa. When my dad sat on the floor of their simple home, he looked around and said, "Where is their stuff?"

"What stuff?" I said.

"Well, their furniture, appliances, TV, laundry etc?"

"This is pretty much it," was my reply.

"Wow," Dad said. "I could sell what's in my garage and buy them out."

What Dad didn't get to know is that the Fatafehi family are as close to us today, some 40 years later, as any of our siblings. Dad could have sold his whole estate and yet never afforded that.

The hospitality of our church families didn't stop there. Many times, fishermen would take our guests for short trips on their boats across to Pangai Island for fishing or snorkelling, or invite them to one of the town restaurants. Out of relative poverty, our visitors were shown exceptional generosity, such was the bond that grew between the two groups. As a result of the gospel at work across the cultural divide, Christian love was shared, creating precious memories for both groups.

Chapter 18

The Pain of Relocation

As the years ticked by, the age and stage of our family brought challenges to the mission in Tonga. We discovered at a very early age that Joel had a congenital muscular dysfunction. When he began high school his ability to function safely and effectively was increasingly difficult. We chose to send him back to do his schooling in New Zealand, but after just a few months realised that was not helpful to him either. We also felt we were at a crossroads for the education of Janita and Gene. Should we stay together until our children were able to function independently of us? Our conclusion was that we should. We needed to relocate our children back into their native society rather than expect them to adapt to our calling to Tonga.

At the same time, we recognised the great potential there was amongst the growing local leadership. Some had ability as Bible teachers, some as evangelists and many as disciple-makers. An issue emerged at a leaders' meeting around open-air preaching, in particular. One of the young men said, "As long as you are amongst us, you must do the open-air preaching."

Admittedly, it had been very much a mission centred around the original teacher/preacher. Along with the family concerns for our children, the thought came powerfully that the time had come to allow local leaders to take responsibility for the vision and function of the mission.

The decision to move away from Tonga was a very painful one, but we believed the time had come.

They could now do open-airs by themselves. There was now strong competency in the national leaders. Leaving behind a country and a people we had been adopted into because of the gospel made us think of Paul's last meeting with the Ephesian elders:

> I commend you to God and to the word of his grace, which is able to build you up and to give you the inheritance among all those who are sanctified. And when he had said these things, he knelt down and prayed with them all. And there was much weeping on the part of all; they embraced Paul and kissed him. (Acts 20:32,36-37)

There was no physical home to return to and, after 15 years out of New Zealand, we had not accumulated resources to draw on, apart from the promise God gave to Elijah ("camp by the brook Cherith and I will feed you there"). But the faith principle was still valid. God's promise is accompanied by God's provision.

We'd certainly been fed in Tonga for 15 years without any lack. Talking to our Tongan family about returning to New Zealand was as traumatic for us as it may have been for them.

Having decided in March 1988 that we would leave Tonga, how would we go about rehabilitating into our homeland? God's providence again – in small print at the bottom of one page of the *Moody Monthly* magazine, we saw an advertisement to study at The Master's Seminary, attached to Grace Community Church in Los Angeles, USA. "What a dream transition," I thought, so quite spontaneously, I flicked off a letter. Three months later, the reply came through by a rather circuitous route. First it went to *Togo*, Africa, and was then readdressed to Tonga! The dean of the seminary, Dr Charles Smith, having considered our years of missionary experience and connections with the Gospel Churches of New Zealand, would allow me to enrol for the B.Th. programme.

We left Tonga in April 1988 and within a couple of months had been given scholarship funding from New Zealand trusts to fly to Sun Valley, Los Angeles. Then to cap it off, Grace Community Church offered a "Ministerial Residency". A big name for a permanent role – 30 hours per week as a pastor to the children's department, with a salary and all seminary expenses paid until the three-year course was completed. Who could have planned such a transition, from mission field to seminary experience then back to our homeland after completion of the degree?

So ended 18 years of absence from New Zealand, planting churches in Tonga then intense seminary training in sync with the life of Grace Community Church. In the years since our return, it has been a great privilege to involve ourselves with Gospel Assemblies in Rotorua and Papatoetoe, and a Tongan church-plant – Amatakiloa Gospel Church in Mangere.

We owe a very deep debt of gratitude to the Brethren Movement of New Zealand (CCCNZ) for all the years of support since our call to mission in 1973.

> Not one word of all the good promises that the Lord had made to the house of Israel had failed; all came to pass. (Joshua 21:45)

Postscript

April 2023

Forty-nine years after we first landed in Tonga, we returned to spend 18 days in Nuku'alofa helping Mobile Mission Maintenance (MMM) and Child Evangelism Fellowship NZ (CEF) in connection with GC3 (Global Connections in Missions) on another valuable project.

Theresa Llorente, who has been working with CEF as part of Tonga Gospel Fellowship for 30 years, suffered significant loss of her home after the suboceanic volcano Hunga Ha'apai had erupted and sent a devastating tsunami to Tongatapu.

Theresa's work has multiplied through most of the denominations as they recognise the importance of teaching truth to children. The Gospel Fellowship churches have been the home base for her work. She has had a deep influence over all these years. Theresa has several strong, influential women around her from many denominations who pray regularly for the impact of the gospel. She has been granted permanent residence; a privilege only given out very sparingly.

The construction of her new house was a wonderful example of New Zealand and Tongan churches working together. While there, we were able to observe the irresistible work of grace in the churches.

One thing we discovered was the disproportionate number of men and women from the Gospel Churches who have found themselves in positions of responsibility in government and private sectors. Disproportionate, in that traditional churches and cults represent significantly higher numbers of the population and could well have been given positions of greater leadership based on that social influence. Instead, it appears positions have been granted based on the merit of the qualifications and personal character of Gospel Church members. It was pointed out to us that a possible reason for this could be the depth of understanding of the true source of wisdom.

Scripture teaches that the outworking of God's grace in individual families means each new generation must "work out their salvation". When there is integrity in the workplace, God rewards accordingly (see Appendix 2).

While purchasing from a large building supplier for Theresa's new house, the manager asked what all the materials were for. Then he enquired about the church where the house was being erected. He said, "That's where E_____ is a leader, right?"

"Exactly," I said.

"Well, of all the businesspeople I deal with in Tonga, he stands out above the rest. He is a man of the highest integrity and reliability."

Perhaps our deepest impressions came from the responses expressed during open worship, familiar to the original Gospel Church format. One after the other, congregants burst out in exuberant and passion-filled praise, something we will no doubt enjoy when gathered around the throne but in an infinitely greater measure. Hymns were selected by one gifted brother and together with the sound of a keyboard, and a hundred worshipful voices, we lifted our hearts in praise. Spontaneous and heartfelt worship of God in these weekly gatherings continues to be a central part of the churches' culture. How blessed we were to see our years of mission in Tonga bearing the fruit of praise to our Great God.

Appendices

Appendix 1

The Gospel We Preach

What is the gospel, that supernatural sound that awakened a small but sincere company of Christians over the 15 years of our mission? Why is it different from the traditional preaching in many Tongan churches?

- The Good News has a supernatural origin. The Bible is the very word of God and as such needs to be given highest honour in the Church. It is pure and wholly true in all it says about man's relationship to God. As people commented soon after the radio sermons began, "Your sermons are directly from the Bible and remain with what the Bible says to the end. No diversions to political or social issues."

    What, then, is the first major issue from this supernatural revelation?

- All people are sinful to the core and as such are unable by any means whatsoever to bridge the gap between God and themselves. All have sinned and fallen short of His standard of fellowship. Isaiah reminded God's people, "Your sins have made a separation between you and your God." Traditional preaching fails to make clear how totally incapable any person is of restoring themselves to God. On the contrary, most people believe the lie that church attendance and taking part in church ordinances will gain them merit towards the prize of life eternal. This principle is clearly demonstrated by the two who went up to the temple to pray (Luke 18:9-14). One was thanking God for the tithes he gave, the fasting he did and that he wasn't like that sinner over there. The other admitted how destitute he was and cried out for mercy. Jesus pointed out this hard truth to the religious elite the same way gospel preachers need to in a Christianised society like Tonga. All are totally corrupt to the heart and unable to be made right with God by their efforts.

Is there a supernatural sound to awaken such a people?

- Jesus is the name that calms our fears and bids our sorrow cease. His name is music to the ears, the music of life and health and peace. But to be clear, "the name" is the nature of Jesus Christ, the Son of God; the name is the character and work of the one and only who can bring us back to God. The beautiful sound is that Christ died for our sin, the just (He), for the unjust (we), that by His death alone we can be reconciled to God. When 'Ofa heard that all his sins could be forgiven on that night in Pātangata, he'd never heard that before, but the powerful Good News reached him, forgave him and changed him into an evangelist from that day til this. When a person agrees with God about his sinfulness and believes in the death, burial and resurrection of Jesus Christ for his sin, he is saved. And so will all who call on the name of the Lord. Strangely and sadly, many preachers in many churches have never heard and believed that beautiful sound. So, people come and are lulled into a deadly sense of security.

Is the sound of the Good News just a one-off experience like attending a concert and being enthralled by a glorious anthem?

- Hearing and believing in the name of Jesus Christ activates God's supernatural power in the person who believes. It's called being "born-again", being born from above.

    How does that newness show up in a life?

    There's often an immediate sense of wonder, of being accepted into God's family. There's often a joy like that of a blind man coming out of darkness into colour, beauty, a new world. But far more than that, this new creature begins to love what God loves, hate what God hates and desires to live the way Jesus lived. Jesus was full of gracious words and good deeds. The Christian then begins the life of good works and good words. All this comes about through hearing and believing the supernatural sound of the gospel.

    How different this transformation is from the fatal idea that a person can do enough good works to deserve forgiveness. To think that is to try to add to the complete work Jesus Christ did on the cross. Doing good works for forgiveness and eternal life is the tragic pathway of all man-made religions. It's the same as much of the religion in Tonga that has minimised these vital truths of scripture, neglected the sinfulness of all people, polluted the perfect work of Jesus Christ, and miscalculated the origins and purpose of good works.

Praise God, the gospel is still the power of God for salvation to the Jew first and also to the whole world. It's this lovely sound that was heard in the hearts of hundreds that began back in 1974 and is still being heard today.

Appendix 2

A Legacy

The following is a sample of positions of responsibility that Tongan Gospel Church people are working in, places where the Christian testimony is being worked out.

Halaleva Gospel Chapel

Tali and Losaline Vakalahi	Senior Managers and Lecturers, Fokololo Technical School
Liuaki and Ana	Ministry of Infrastructure
Aisea Vave	Ministry of Justice
Viliami Pohiva	Human Resource Manager, Tonga Airposts Ltd
Kalolaine Pohiva	Chief Administration Officer, Tonga Communication Corporation
Filimone Pohiva	Commercial pilot training, NZ
Eneio Leilani	Consultant and Lecturer, Teachers Training Pre-school Education
Loiloi Kris	Department of Environment

Peni Leilani	Mechanical Engineer, Ministry of Infrastructure
Fifita Vakalahi	Senior Officer, ANZ Tonga
Siosiua 'Ahotau Pohiva	Diploma of Nursing
Tevita Vakalahi	Tonga Police
Manu Fukofuka	Master's degree, Ministry of Finance
Aloisia Pohiva	Radio and Youth for Christ Tonga

Touliki Gospel Chapel

'Esafe Tokai	Retired Acting Deputy CEO, Revenue and Customs
Sitia Tokai	Assistant Secretary, Ombudsman Office
'Otukolo Tokai	Ministry of Meteorology, Energy, Information
Sione Tokai	Principal Officer, Ministry of Finance
Lusi Tokai	Legal Officer, Ministry of Meteorology, Energy, Information
Siu Fukofuka	Principal Registrar, Prime Minister's Office
Gladys Fukofuka	Deputy CEO Human Resources, Ministry of Finance

Vaini Fatafehi	Sales Officer, office equipment retail company
Fatai Unufe	Sales Manager, OE company
Melisa Feʻofaʻaki	Sales Officer, Nukuʻalofa Medical Clinic
Tilisa Fukofuka	Medical school, USA
Sioeli Pohiva	LLB student, USP University
Tapui Petelo	Tonga Communications Company
Ailine Tokai	Tertiary Institute of Higher Education, Ministry of Education
Viliami Tongamana	Project Manager, Ministry of Meteorology, Energy, Information
Fusi Tokai	Customs, Security
Viliami Fatafehi	Retired, US Peace Corps

Manuka Gospel Chapel

Fine Ngalu	Retired Senior Customs Officer
Timote Polovili	Coach, Tonga Football Federation

For I determined to know nothing among you except Jesus Christ and him crucified. (1 Corinthians 2:2 NASB)

Appendix 3

Documents

On the following pages are reproductions of documents related to key aspects of the story told in this book.

1. Report by Mr Foster Crane, 1971.
2. Registration of Gospel Fellowship Lease for Church Building and Residence for Pastor, 1972.
3. Report by Dr Vautier after his visit to Tonga, 1973.
4. Commendation for Missionary Service, January 1974.
5. Tongan Visa to Reside, January 1974.
6. Request from two of the original elders for a visa extension for the McNae family, January 1974.
7. Tonga Gospel Fellowship Trust document, created by Dr Vautier and affirmed by the Tongan leadership team, September 1975.
8. Tongan Visa renewal, December 1978.
9. A letter written by a noble warning Naisa about visiting "his territory", November 1986.

Appendix 3 | 239

The Kingdom

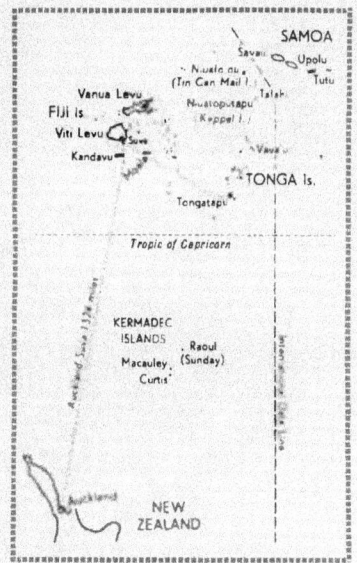

# of Tonga

This page and overleaf next six pages: Document 1.

THE KINGDOM OF TONGA

(The following report relating to Mr F. Crane's recent visit to Tonga was discussed at the Workers' and Elders' Conference last weekend and it was agreed by all present that it should be printed and distributed to N.Z. Assemblies for their prayerful interest and fellowship).

"Of recent months there has been an obvious exercise re the spiritual needs of Tonga and the possibility of a G.L.O. visit and the establishment of a local assembly witness. At the request of brethren concerned I recently spent three weeks in the Islands with a view to investigating the possibility of furthering these projects.

It was by no means an easy assignment and I was much cast on the Lord for guidance. The only Tongan I knew, was a boy who had attended our Primary School in Suva some years ago, though I had quite a list of names of people who were known by others (in N.Z. and Fiji) or who had been contacted by correspondence. My enquiries too, were limited in that many of the people I endeavoured to contact were unable to speak English, hence interpretation was necessary.

Tonga has a population of about 80,000 people who live in three distinct Island Groups — Tongatapu, Ha'apai, and Vava'u. The majority live in the former Group, Nuku'alofa being the Capital town. It is a land of religious confusion with 14 different denominations and religious bodies. Methodists are divided into three Groups and Mormon "churches" are in every village.

My first move was to contact a few evangelical leaders (European and Tongan — whose names I had been given) of the Free Weselyan Church to sound out their re-actions to a G.L.O. visit — among these was a keen Tongan, Senetuli Koloi, and the local Scripture Union Committee. The S.U. Committee is doing a splendid work in translating S.U. notes into Tongan and they are finding a ready demand for these — I sat in on one of their Committee meetings. Senetuli asked me to address a large group of his "lay" preachers on "Baptism and the Sacraments" (from a Methodist viewpoint!) I agreed to speak provided he let me speak on the gospel only and we had quite a profitable evening. To the majority of Tongans the blessings of God are somehow wrapped up in the "sacraments" of the church and can only be received through the services of Clergyman, Priest or Mormon Elders.

All of these were sympathetic to a G.L.O. visit provided literature was confined to the Scriptures, evangelical tracts, Scripture Union Notes, etc., and was carried out per medium of the Methodist Youth Fellowships. There was obvious reluctance to the use of any literature relating to baptism and the church, or that may upset the status quo of the Free Weselyan Church.

As English is not as well known in Tonga as in Fiji, most literature would have to be in the Tongan language and workers would need to have guides and interpreters. None of the Wesleyans, however, were helpful in the offer of accommodation. The only satisfactory answer to the problem is the establishment of a local centre within Tonga free from denominational restrictions and that is able to provide accommodation. This leads me to the consideration of a small Group of believers in Nuku'alofa known as the "FANGA FELLOWSHIP". (Fanga is the name of a local suburb in Nuku'alofa).

The history of the Fellowship is briefly as follows. About six years ago in the Vava'u Group (160 miles to the North) two men, Fine Tane and Setaleki Afuha'amango were saved and baptized through the instrumentality of a passing Evangelist from Pago-pago in American Samoa — they have no idea with what church or mission he was associated. Not knowing what church to join, these two commenced a work of their own in Vava'u and called it the "Neiafu Baptist Fellowship" simply because they practiced believers' baptism. (They assure me they have no connection with Baptists as such, though, along with other visitors, one or two Baptists have visited them). Both men continued to support themselves (as they still do) but declare that their main object in life is to "preach the gospel in the darkness".

Later they moved to Nuku'alofa and rented a place for meetings but, owing to their extreme poverty, they could not pay the rent and had to give it up. They moved to another place but met with much opposition from the established churches so returned to Vava'u. Last year they returned to the Capital and made another start holding meetings in Seta's "house" — a small 20' x 15' room that is literally falling to pieces. Here they dropped the word "Baptist" and simply called themselves the "Fanga Fellowship".

I had the names of these two men on my list and, remarkably enough, I met Seta on the water-front the first day I arrived and had a long talk with him. He told me about the Fellowship and asked me to speak at it on Sunday night and to this I agreed. It was not until later when checking my list that I discovered that this was the "key" man I had been asked to contact!

About 50 adults and children managed to find seating (on the floor) in the small room. Most of these were outsiders — there are very few baptized members. Fine opened the meeting and he was followed by a local "elder" who gave a short talk. On account of the poverty there were only two hymn books so Fine read each verse before it was sung. The singing was quite fantastic, deep, natural harmony which filled the small room.

I then spoke by interpretation, after which the Fellowship Members took the Lord's Supper. This was passed around by Fine to the members who simply knelt where they were in the congregation: the bread was cut in pieces and separate cups used (real wine). The supper is observed once a month. Finally the meeting was opened for Prayer in which Seta's wife took part. All present were then invited to a meal (Tongan) prepared each Sunday night by Seta and his wife out of their extreme poverty. They apologized for the fact that they possessed only one spoon and knife for the whole family of nine children: as guest of honour I was given first use of the spoon and it was then passed round to others who wished to eat with it!

Without wishing to become too involved, I spent most of my time with these folk, speaking at their meetings and observing their activities. At their request I later left the Boarding House where I was staying and spent 11 days living Tongan fashion with them in their homes. Many hours I spent sitting on the floors discussing the things of God, sharing their meagre, yet warm hearted hospitality.

Some aspects of their church activities, as mentioned above, were unusual and, to some extent unscriptural, but, having had no contact with outside evangelical Christians or assembly practices, it was perhaps to be expected that they would carry on the practices with which they were previously familiar. Against this however, were three clear desires on their part —

(a) To meet on a strictly non-denominational basis recognizing only true believers as members of the church of God, avoiding any name that may suggest they were forming a new denomination.

(b) To preach the gospel of the grace of God. They have meetings in homes or open air on week nights which may continue till midnight. As they have no transport, members have to walk long distances.

(c) To baptize converts by immersion. Five were baptized in the sea (by Fine) while I was with them — four men and a young married woman — and I have never seen a baptism carried out in a more dignified and gracious manner; the dear girl walked slowly from the sea singing quietly to herself with tears rolling down her face. I do not think there was a dry eye in the whole group.

These five were not baptized because of any prompting on my part — I had not mentioned the subject to them. They (and others who will be following them in a week or two) were already ready, but rather fearful of the obvious "reproach" of publicly identifying themselves with Christ and the Fellowship. However, the knowledge that similar Groups of believers in Fiji, Samoa, and other places were preaching the same gospel and facing the same testings, gave the whole Group, and these in particular, the spiritual boost they needed at a time when morale was low.

At first I found Seta, their leader, somewhat objectionable. He was converted later in life and has a brusque, out-spoken manner, somewhat untidy in appearance (he told me he wanted to live and dress as a Tongan — not as a dressed-up Pastor or Minister!). By reason of his good knowledge of English, however, he is an aggressive leader of the Fellowship. He possesses land in the country and could live quite comfortably but insists that he and his wife gave up the land and came to Nuku'alofa for the one object of helping the Fellowship and preaching the gospel. What little money he earns from the selling of curios to the tourists he declares goes entirely in the Lord's work and they look to the Lord to meet their needs.

Seta's wife, Tulaki, is a very devoted, Godly woman with nine children of her own (some are away from home) yet she still takes into her "home" occasional needy or orphaned children from outside families. One of these (a sick child of seven weeks) died while I was there and I attended the funeral. Literally all they possess is shared with others. While Seta and I were in Vava'u (below) she gave away her second to last dress and her husband's second to last shirt! He complimented her on her action. I had some used men's shirts with me so passed them on, but I heard later that, with the exception of one shirt for her husband, she had given them all away! One day recently the whole family went foodless. To see these things happening before my very eyes had quite a shattering effect on my desire for comfort and ease and I felt rebuked and humbled in their presence.

Fine is a deeply spiritual man and obviously much burdened for the spiritual welfare of the Fellowship. He spends some time fasting before each baptism in order to discern the mind of the Lord. He does most of the preaching and teaching. His English is limited but he appears to be thoroughly genuine and meets with much opposition from the established churches.

It is hard to avoid the conviction that their motives are right and that they are genuinely seeking to do the Lord's will under most trying circumstances.

I took Seta with me on a five day visit to the Northern Group of Islands at Vava'u. This involved a 16 hour sea trip in quite a comfortable boat that makes the round trip twice weekly. Half way it passes through the beautiful Ha'apai Group, here and there stopping to pick up or put down passengers in small sailing ships that drew alongside. To cruise slowly through these magnificent Islands (at one time I counted twenty in sight) is a millionaire's dream but to date their natural charm and peace is undisturbed by tourist hotels. I had persons to contact in Ha'apai but shipping schedules made it impossible for me to stay.

At Vava'u I stayed with Sisi Lopeti, the sole surviving member of the original Neiafu Fellowship. Aged 62, he was saved only two years ago and baptized by Fine. He bravely holds a Fellowship meeting in his home (assisted by his son) on two nights a week but few attend. Though his knowledge of English is very poor, I found him to be a most sincere man with a genuine love for the Lord. The Bible is his only text Book.

There is another small Group of believers a few miles from Sisi's place and we had a meeting with them one night. I gathered they were more of a separated Wesleyan Group (unbaptized) but with a desire to know more of the Word of God.

Another day we went by launch on a two-hour trip to the Island of Nuga to visit a baptized woman — a likeable soul who fasts every Friday and has a women's meeting in her house the same day. The return trip in a very small launch was quite exciting and I got a wetting from spray owing to head winds in the open sea — it took three hours.

After the gospel meeting referred to above, the Fellowship members asked if I would discuss witht them their main problem — the need of a more suitable meeting place; it was obvious that their witness could never make much progress in Seta's collapsing house. One of their adherents had offered to let them have a block of three acres in quite a good locality in a suburb of Nuku'alofa on condition that they gave him a "boat"! They had, in fact, accepted his offer and had commenced clearing the land of bush.

At their request I later went to thte land and watched the women plaiting coconut leaves for the walls of a temporary meeting place, the men were clearing trees and planting taro and yams. I discussed the purchase conditions with Sefo (the owner) and the elders, but as nobody had any idea as to the type of "boat" Sefo wanted, I advised him to set a price and this he eventually did at $2,400.

A day or so after this, however, radio Tonga announced that the first test bore for Tongan oil was to be sunk a bare $\frac{1}{4}$ mile from the land in question. Whether this influenced Sefo or not we do not know, but when Seta and I were in Vava'u he informed the elders that his price had risen to $6000.00! and all the fellowship possessed was six dollars.

Unlike all outside missions who pour tens of thousands of dollars into the country, the believers had no outside contacts and were practically centless. It says something for their courage that they had commenced clearing the land without the faintest idea of where the money was to come from. They had some vague hope that some of their members may be able to go to New Zealand to earn money. Was it a coincidence that on the evening of this discussion I read almost casually in Ezra 6. 8. "I make a decree what ye shall do to the elders of these Jews, for the building of this house of God; that of the King's goods even of the tribute beyond the river forthwith expenses be given unto these men that they be not hindered."

Our boat arrived back from Vava'u at midnight on Tuesday the 14th and I was due to return to Suva on the 15th. The elders, however, wanted further discussion with me, so they came together the same night at 1 a.m. and we continued our talk till 3.30 a.m. — five of us sitting on the floor of Seta's house around a smoky kerosene light, my head reeling! I did not feel I could leave them in their tangle, so cancelled my flight for several days.

Eventually "we" secured an acre adjoining Sefos' land — a very nice piece of land for 1,500 dollars — 500 dollars deposit, and called a Solicitor for advice. The first thing he asked was who was going to pay the 500 dollars deposit.

I could no longer avoid the fact that I had to make a decision — either we support these people or we don't. I was greatly burdened with the responsibility that weighed upon me, and just longed for another responsible brother with whom to consult — but there was none. I was not altogether happy about their activities and was a little fearful of the "risk" involved.

Against this, however, three important factors were apparent.

1. The remarkable way in which the Lord appeared to be leading — the prayers of brethren in N.Z. — my unexpected meeting with Seta the day I arrived — my sudden appearance into the fellowship group almost the very day they were facing a land problem. They looked upon me as a direct answer to their prayers — an 'angel' from God who had, almost literally dropped into their midst from Heaven. Who was I to resist the work of God? If it was His doing, could He not care for the future?

2. The fact that this was a wholly indigenous move from within the country. Any attempt to establish assembly work from without would almost certainly have met with Government refusal. It was a very definite crack in the wall, that may never open a second time.

3. It was a clear answer to the G.L.O. problem — a definite permanent centre of activity within the country from which the Gospel may radiate, and literature be distributed, without any compromise to Biblical truth. Guides and interpreters are available. The Fellowship is most happy to welcome visitors from overseas, and has agreed that 2 permanent rooms be added to the proposed meeting-house for workers.

With all these things in mind I told the Solicitor that I — "we"? — would accept responsibility for the initial payment.

On the final Sunday night I met with the Fellowship again, and we endeavoured to get the work on a more stable footing, and adopt a plan of campaign. It was agreed —

(a) To recognize a definite eldership of the fellowship.
(b) To call the new development "The HALA'LEVA GOSPEL FELLOWSHIP" — their suggestion — Hala'leva in the name of the district. Trustees were appointed and a simple constitution prepared.
(c) To open a Bank account under the same name.
(d) To erect a new meeting place of 40 feet by 20 feet, with adjoining rooms for visitors as the Lord enables. A year or so ago, a move was commenced to build a boat to reach out to other Islands. Trees were cut and the logs taken to a mill, but for lack of finance they were not sawn into timber. In the meantime the boat project has been abandoned, and it is hoped to mill the timber for the proposed new Hall as soon as finance is available. Cost of the building will probably be about 3000 dollars. I drew them a rough sketch as a suggested design to follow.

For the benefit of interested brethren, and assemblies overseas, I suggest the following —

1. Establish a "Tonga Development fund" in Suva, with the object of

assisting in the land purchase, the building programme, the provision of Tongan literature, local workers, subsidies to Tongan attending our proposed Bible School in Suva, and related activities.
2. Assist a couple of single Maori young men with a knowledge of carpentry — or a married man with his wife — to go to Tonga and help with the building. They should be able to give spiritual help and counsel also. This is quite an urgent matter. The Fellowship will provide immediate accommodation — Tongan fashion. Visitors permits are available for six months. I have application forms for any who are exercised.
I suggest Maori brethren on account of their racial kinship with Tongans. The presence of Europeans is inclined to create the impression that a new "Papalagi" (white man's) denomination is being established.
3. With the completion of the building a Maori evangelist could hold a campaign.
4. Two or three G.L.O. workers (Maoris preferably) could follow this over a further six month period. Tongan literature is being prepared in the meantime — a girl there is already working on a translation of the Young Christian booklet. The feeling is that literature should be distributed freely in order to avoid identification with J.Ws. For the guidance of visitors Mini-skirts for girls and short trousers for men, are definitely out of place. Given the use of a van — and possibly a projector — open-air meetings could be held anywhere on the Island. It is only 20 miles long with roads to all townships.
5. Visiting Bible teachers — possibly our own local Fiji workers — could pay occasional visits. The Fellowship needs a great deal of instruction concerning Local Church order and practice, but I feel they are willing to learn.
6. Keen Tongan Christians could be encouraged and assisted to attend the Bible School in Suva for three months. Several are already interested, but practically all expenses would have to be paid by us. The future development of the work will largely depend on these latter young people."
We commend this work to your prayerful and practical fellowship.

Yours in His Service,

J. FOSTER CRANE

P.S. For the information of any who are interested, an account has been opened with the Bank of N.Z., Suva, known as the "Tonga Gospel Fellowship Fund". Correspondence in the meantime should be addressed to Mr A. Crane, 45 Nailuva Rd., Suva.

Fika: L.3/2/1.

MINISTRY OF LANDS & SURVEY,
NUKUʻALOFA, TONGA.

Kau Talasiti,
Siasi Gospel Fellowship,
Halaleva,
KOLOFOʻOU

3 ʻAkosi, 1972.

Kau Talasiti,

    ʻOku ou fakaʻapaʻapa mo fakaha heni kuo tali ʻe he Houʻeiki fakataha Kapineti ʻa ʻEne ʻAfio ʻi he tuʻutuʻuni Kapineti Fika 810 ʻo e ʻaho 24 Siulai, 1972 hoʻomou kole lisi tuʻunga fale lotu ki he konga ʻapi ʻi Halaleva, Koloʻoʻou.

2.   ʻE kamata lau e lisi ni mei he ʻaho ʻe lesisita ai, pea ko hono fakaikiiki ʻo e lisi ni ʻoku pehe :-

    Lesiʻi   - Gospel Fellowship
    Lesoa   - Kalauni
    Lahi ʻo e ʻapi- OA.1R.24P.
    Taimi   - Taʻu e 50.
    Totongi   - $6.40 ki he taʻu.
    Faʻahinga ʻo e lisi - Tuʻunga fale lotu.

Faka'apa'apa atu,

Minisita Fonua.

Sr:tt.

This page and opposite: Document 2.

15

C
O
P
Y

Fika: F.3/2/1.

11 Sepitema, 1972.

Kau Talasiti,
Gospel Fellowship,
HALALEVA.

Kau Talasiti,

    'Oku ou faka'apa'apa mo fakaha heni kuo tali 'e he Kapineti 'i he tu'utu'uni Kapineti Fika 1016 'o e 'aho 6 Sepitema, 1972 'a ho'omou kole lisi e konga 'api kolo 'i he tofi'a 'o e Pule'anga 'i Halaleva.

2.   'E toki kamata lau e lisi ni mei he 'aho 'e lesisita ai, pea ko hono fakaikiiki 'oku pehe ni -

Lesoa	-	Kalauni
Lesi'i	-	Gospel Fellowship
Lahi e 'api	-	1R.24P.
Taimi	-	Ta'u e 50.
Totongi	-	T$30.00
Fa'ahinga 'o e lisi	-	Nofo'anga Faifekau.

Faka'apa'apa atu,

(Sgd) Tuita

Minisita Fonua.

SF:tt.

A NEW CHAPEL FOR TONGA

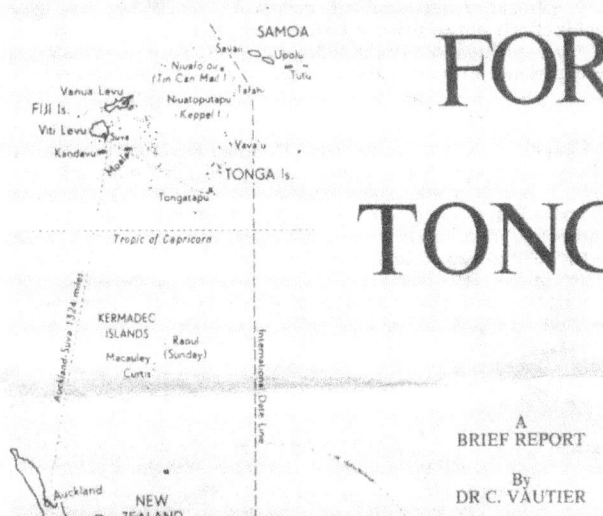

A BRIEF REPORT
By
DR C. VAUTIER

The chapel hall takes shape.

Following four pages: Document 3.

BRIEF REPORT ON TONGAN POSITION   1973

My wife and I visited Tonga from September 11-22. We were met by Dr Victor Wilson of Ashburton, and taken to the site where the chapel buildings are taking shape under Bernie Tolmie who is doing a magnificent job under fairly difficult conditions. Dr Wilson has been tireless in his efforts in procuring materials and organising the project as well as giving a spiritual lead in the young assembly. He is contributing a wealth of experience in control and management on the business side.

The Chapel: This is an attractively designed building in concrete blocks. The main chapel hall is approximately 30' x 40' with sufficient stud height to permit a mezzanine floor in the front (for the future if required) and a first floor over the Bible Class room and other rooms at the rear (about 30' x 18'). Behind the main building is attached a flat (23' x 17') and it is proposed to have a lean-to built for shelter for a car or vehicle. Before we left the roof was on the entire building, this achievement being partly due to the effort of our brother Murray Smith (of Ashburton) who spent his annual holiday there with a hammer in his hand.

Progress: Quite a bit is yet to be done to complete the entire project. The floor, joinery, painting, plumbing, electrical fittings, front porch, glazing, internal partitioning, ceiling and paintwork have yet to be paid for and completed. The work done to hand and the materials involved including glass have been paid for, but the amount required to complete the job is estimated to be in the vicinity of $4,500.

This is the sum that is required. It is not desirable that this young assembly "borrow" in the form of loans or mortgages, as the members are very poor, and will be taxed to meet the ground-lease rental of $36.00 p.a. The total floor area is over 2,500 sq. ft. and the entire cost of the building project will be under $3.00 a sq. ft. This has been made possible only by the untiring efforts of those who have worked so hard there, and are continuing to give unstinted help.

The oversight of the expenditure is under Dr Wilson's immediate control. The funds are administered through a Tonga Fellowship account at the Bank of New Zealand, Suva, Fiji, operated by our brother Foster Crane who has been so instrumental in initiating and guiding the total effort in Tonga. He is working jointly with Dr Wilson in planning and control of the outlays and building project, apart from giving spiritual help and guidance. Funds as required are transferred by joint signature to a Post Office account in Tonga.

The needs: These have been set out in some detail for your sympathetic knowledge and information. The buildings (chapel and extensions) are on a front lease of 2/5th of an acre, and another lease of the rear section of another 2/5th of an acre is held for building a residence for a fulltime worker or visiting brethren who may come to help forward the spiritual work in Tonga. The leases are for 50 years and from the Crown and cost $1,500. They carry an annual rental of $6.00 and $30.00 respectively. (The leases themselves are a wonderful provision, for long-term leases are almost impossible to obtain in Tonga).

The spiritual position: The assembly consists of two New Zealand brothers and a sister, and a number of Tongan believers. Of these, two or three are older brothers and several younger men and children. One older sister is a particularly fine Christian woman with a young growing family. She is helping very materially in loving care for those working on the project. One young Tongan brother (married), Paul Topou, acted as interpreter during the course of the meetings held here. He is a fine young man with considerable spiritual potential. Unfortunately he is being transfered to Vava'u for 6 months but even this is no doubt under the Lord's land, for there are believers in the northern group of islands. It is considered that there is urgent need for a married couple to be permanently resident in Tonga, to learn the language and help this young assembly forward in the truth. At the same time it is highly desirable that future provision be made to accommodate mature persons who would be prepared to be resident and help for short periods. Already a most suitable young couple have written, expressing interest and willingness to go to Tonga.

Meanwhile a further eight young people from Nuku'alofa and Vava'u expect to be attending the Coral Coast Bible School in Fiji in February 1974. These will all have to come at the expense of the Assembly and the Bible School - an investment really worth while. Another need is suitable literature, and to this end we aim to get some of Foster Crane's booklets translated into Tongan for use and distribution.

May we draw your attention to the articles in the "Treasury" about Tonga — that of October 1969 and September 1972 where objectives and progress were reported. Much has been achieved, much is being achieved, and much remains to be done. The Lord is blessing and working in Tonga. May we be workers together with Him.

CLYDE VAUTIER,
20 OCTOBER, 1973

Appendix 3 | 251

The Bible class room at the Left and the 24' x 17' flat to the right

Mrs Wilson and Sione Finau

Fine Taue (one of the elders there) on the R. and one of the young men who are helping in spare time.

Where the assembly has been meeting.

Dr Victor Wilson.

Tulaki and four of her children.

Commendation. Mr & Mrs Graeme McNAE

17 Brunner street,
Nelson.
4 January, 1974.

Treasurers,
N.Z.Missionary Funds
Palmerston North.

Dear Brethren,

On 18 December, 1973, the members of the oversight of the Nelson Christian Brethren Assembly, commended our brother and sister, Mr. and Mrs. Graeme McNae to the work of the Lord in Tonga. This was subsequently endorsed by the assembly.

Graeme, Colleen, and baby Joel left New Zealand for Tonga on 4 January.

Will you please advise the news editor, the Treasury, of these facts.

Should any assembly or individual like to obtain a copy of future letters from our brother and sister from Tonga, would they please inform me.

Yours in Christ, on behalf of the Christian Brethren Assembly,

M. Brown.

Certified true photocopy of original letter received in the office of Missionary Funds (NZ) Incorporated in 1974.
FOR AND ON BEHALF OF
MISSIONARY FUNDS (N.Z.) INCORPORATED
TRUSTEE

This page and opposite: Document 4.

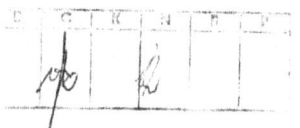

le G. McNAE

FENTON PARK GOSPEL CHAPEL,
P.O. Box 1257,
ROTORUA,
14th. March, 1974.

The Secretary,
"The Treasury",
P.O. Box 74,
PALMERSTON NORTH.

Dear Sirs,

    Would you kindly publish in "The Treasury" that Graham (Graeme) and Colleen McNae, who were commended by the Nelson Assembly to Tonga, are also commended from the Fenton Park Gospel Chapel, Rotorua, as this was Colleen's home Assembly before her marriage.

    Also, if you have not already been advised by Brother V.G. Hooper, who is going on an overseas trip, that he has resigned the position of Assembly correspondent in my favour, that is :-

        Neville R. Forlong,
        P.O. Box 1257,
        Rotorua,
If 'phone numbers required   86232 (home)   84143 (bus)

    Yours on behalf of the above Assembly,

    Neville R. Forlong
        Secretary.

Certified true photocopy of original letter received in the office of Missionary Funds (NZ) Incorporated in 1974.

FOR AND ON BEHALF OF
MISSIONARY FUNDS (N.Z.) INCORPORATED

                TRUSTEE

Tonga Gospel Fellowship,
P.O. Box 848,
Nuku'alofa.

To the Royal Cabinet Meeting of
His Majesty King Tupou IV

We hereby appeal to the Highest Royal Cabinet of His
Majesty for our Brother in Christ from New Zealand, by
the name of Mr. Graeme McNae.

We request that Mr. McNae, who has recently completed a
course of intensive Bible study and practical training at
a Bible College in New Zealand, be permitted to reside in
Tonga with his wife and child. We would like him to act
as a preacher and helper in the Lords work in our Fellowship,
which was registered with the Tongan Government known at
"Tonga Gospel Fellowship in 1973."

Mr. McNae and his wife are both very proficient with many
musical instruments and have already been enjoyed by all
our fellowship. We have also seen their willingness and
competence to help in as many practical ways as they can,
e.g. Building, clothing, minor medical help, teaching music
and handwork.

We know they will be a great help not only to our fellowship
but to all the people of Tonga.

This request is made by all the members of the "Tongan
Gospel Fellowship and especially the trustees - Mr. Leta
and Georgie.

....
(Setaleki Afuha'amango)

This page and opposite: Document 5.

C O P Y

Box 848
Nuku'alofa
Tonga.

30.1.74

The Chief Police of Immigration,
Nuku'alofa,
TONGA.

Dear Sir,

For the last five years my wife and I have been actively involved in christian work particularly among the youth. My wife's father, Mr.C.H. Hilton is founder and direction of "Kiwi Ranches", NZ. through which 15,000 young people pass each year. The weekly camps which these young people attend are designed to educate in spiritual matters and make better citizens for New Zealand. Mr. Hilton is widely know throughout New Zealand and Australia as an Evangelistic preacher and Minister. My wife and I have spent many years assisting in this work.

Our interest in the christian work in Tonga began in 1972 when we sponsored two Tongan students to attend Coral Coast Bible School in Fiji. Our interest in the Tongan people grew and after much serious consideration, during a bible study course we attended last tear, and having a knowledge of the spiritual need in this fellowship, we decided to make themselves available to this church and to the Kingdom of Tonga.

Having been here three weeks we have already seen many ways by which we could help the people.

1. Ministering the Word of God, especially in the Tonga Gospel Fellowship.

2. Teaching to play a number of musical instruments eg. piano, organ, saxaphone, xylophone guitar.

3. Assisting with the building of small homes.

4. Assisting in scientific work with the Department of Agriculture having had five years training and experience in a research laboratory.

5. Mrs. McNac is willing to teach and assist with sewing and handcrafts to as many as she is able.

6. Treatment of minor medical needs of the people in our area.

We humbly request that we be permitted to reside in Tonga for three years and devote ourselves to the people, the land and to God. We hereby pledge to faithfully obey all authorities of the Land and will be happy to accept your decision on this request.

Yours sincerely,

(G.A.McNac) C.M.McNac.

Tonga Gospel Fellowship,
P.O. Box 848,
Nuku'alofa.

29th January, 1974.

Ki he Fakataha 'Eiki 'a 'Ene 'afio, Tupou 1V,

'Oku mau faka'apa'apa mo kole heni ki he Fakataha 'Eiki na tu'unga 'i homau tokoua fakalotu ko Mr. Monae mei New Zealand. 'Oku mau kole atu ke mou anga'ofa ke fakangofua'i 'a e tokotaha ni ke ne hoko ia kohomau taki fakalotu, koe'uhi kou ne 'osi ako fakatohi-tapu 'i he ako'anga fakatohitapu 'i New Zealand. Pea 'oku na 'i heni mo hono mali mo 'ene ki'i tamasi'i, ko 'emau 'a'ahi mai kia kimautolu, tu'unga matu'a 'oku fakatefito ki ai 'a e Lotu (pe) Siasi Kosipeli 'i Tonga ni. 'Oku maka tu'unga 'a e faka- tangi ni koe'uhi 'oku na fu'u fakatou 'aonga 'aupito 'i he ngaahi me'a lahi 'o 'ikai ke ngata pe 'i he me'a fakalotu, ka koe ngaahi ngaue fakatu'asino foki, pea 'oku mau tui pau 'e 'aonga lahi 'a e ongo matu'a ni ki he kaha'u 'o Tonga ni, 'o 'ikai ke ngata pe 'iate kimautolu mo 'emau fanga ki'i fanau, ka koe tokolahi foki 'o kimautolu to'u tupu 'o e fonua ni. 'Okumau fiefia ke nau ako 'i he ngaahi me'a lea 'aia kuo 'i Tonga ni moe ongo matu'a ni. Ko e taha foki 'eni 'o ha langa fonua mo'oni ma'ae Pule'anga 'o Tupou 1V mo Hou'eiki, 'okapau 'e Fakafiemalie ki he Fakataha 'Eiki na 'a e kole ni. 'Oku mau faka'apa'apa atu moe loto fie talangofua mo'oni. Pea koku tefito 'a e tohi ni ki he matu'a Tonga 'aia na'a nau fokotu'u mo langa 'a e Siasi ni 'i he Konga kokekole 'oku 'iloa ko Halaleva.

Faka'apa'apa atu,

Setaleki Afuha'amango

Siaosi Pohahau

(Ko e ongo Sevaniti talangofua
ma'ae Pule'anga 'o Tupou mo
Hou'eiki).

5 Sept 1975

TONGA GOSPEL FELLOWSHIP TRUST

1. THE name of the Trust is "Tonga Gospel Fellowship Trust", and is hereinafter termed "the Trust".

2. THE address of the Trust is P.O. Box 848, Nuku'alofa, Tonga.

3. OBJECTS

THE objectives for which the Trust is incorporated are:—

(a) To provide, procure maintain and administer Trust property in the Kingdom of Tonga for the purpose of the furtherance of the Gospel of God and the teaching of His Word and for the support and advancement of Christian beliefs and practices as set out in Schedule A attached hereto.

(b) To carry out such other works and purposes of a religious nature as are charitable in the legal sense and as the Trust may think fit to perform.

(c) To purchase, take on lease or exchange, hire or otherwise acquire lands, buildings, and any real or personal estate or other property, equipment, facilities or physical assets whatsoever, or any interest in the same respectively, provided the use of such is consistent with the main objectives of the Trust.

(d) To engage in any activity or to do any act, function, operation, commission including entering into any commercial, legal or other business contract, arrangement, or agreement whatsoever, provided the same is consistent with the furtherance of the main objectives of the Trust.

(e) To aid, help, assist or advance the work of any missionary, missionaries, ministers of the Word, preachers of the Gospel of God, by making available to the same any or all of the properties, lands, buildings, equipment or any other facilities or other resources owned by the Trust, provided such work is consistent with the main objectives of the Trust.

(f) To hire, engage, use or employ auditors, secretaries, treasurers, agents, solicitors or other persons for the purpose of carrying out the objects of the Trust.

(g) To receive and take any gift of money or property, to act or be appointed as administrator or executor or trustee of the estate of any deceased person or persons, and to incorporate into the Trust or its title deeds if necessary or desirable any realty or property situate anywhere in the world.

(h) To carry on any form of business or undertaking whatsoever which may directly or indirectly assist the objects for which the Trust is established.

(i) To do any of the above things as principals, trustees or agents and to do all such other things as are incidental or conducive to the attainment of the above objects or any of them.

This page: Document 7.

Box 848,
Nuku'alofa.
Tonga.
17.11.78.

The Honourable Minister of Police,
Police Headquarters.
Nuku'alofa.

Dear Sir,

    We humbly request your permission for the extension of the residence of Mr & Mrs Graeme McNae in Tonga. They have been working as missionaries in our church, Tonga Gospel Fellowship, for nearly five years now and it is our wish that they continue working with us in the preaching of the Gospel and encouragement in our christian lives.

    We humbly ask that they be permitted to reside for another period of three years.

Yours faithfully,

Trustees; S. 'Afuha'amango.

'O Fatafehi.

This page and opposite: Document 8.

IMM.1/21.V.3.

Immigration Dept.,
OFFICE OF THE MINISTER OF POLICE
NUKU'ALOFA, TONGA.

21 December, 1978.

Setaleki AFUHA'AMANGO,
P.O. Box 848,
NUKU'ALOFA.

Tangata'eiki,

    'Oku ou faka'apa'apa kae 'oatu 'a e fakahoha'a ni fekau'aki pea mo e kole fakaloloa ngofua 'a Mr. Graeme McNAE mo hono ki'i famili. 'Oku ou fie fakaha atu heni kuo tali 'a e kole fakaloloa 'o e ngofua 'a Mr. McNAE pea mo hono ki'i famili'i he ta'u koia 'oku fai mai kiai 'a e kole pea 'e fakaloloa fakata'u taha ia.

    'Amanaki pe 'oku mahino atu 'a e fakahoha'a ni.

                  Faka'apa'apa atu,

                    CIP. 'AHOME'E
       O.C. IMMIGRATION DEPARTMENT

'A/ht

FOTU

Leimatu'a
'Vava'u
12/11/86

Laisa,

Mālō male 'ae ngaue mei hena pea 'eku
tau fakamālō a 'Eiki he 'Otua.
Koe tohi ke'eni kuo fai'eni pe he 'eku
tui 'eku ta'e ae me'a fakatauhi fonua
mo fakafamili. 'Eku fai ai 'ae ta'e fiemohonaki
pikaitoki mo loto, Ka hoku peha tatau pe a
Ului mo Satani 'eku 'ou peha 'eku to na talan-
gata'a ki ate au he Neu osi lea 'eku
'ikai teu loto keu alu ki he loto
Kosipeli Neongo ka'e lotu pe a kihe Sisu
e taha Ka 'eku 'ikai teu sai ia he tau
Movetevete he 'eku pau ko teu fai pe
'i laumalie mo Meoni. Koia ko 'eku tohi
atu o fakamālō atu kapau kuo aonga ha
me'a ki hoku peha pea malō ka 'eku 'ikai
teu loto keha hanga o ka'e o fakataumu'a
mo paoa hoku tuenga meiha 'eku fanau
kecahi 'eku 'ou ae Me'a Mahalo 'eku tau taa
fiemohinoaki ai. Ko Ului kona 'eku lahi ihe
fanau (ea) pea kona e Fotu ihe Kahau tauhi
fonua pea kohona fatongia ke tauhi kie
Kakai ke ma'au oua e Movetevete ke h
fotu pe e taha pea 'eku 'ikai teu loto
keu Mavahe ake 'o taa'i taaki taumu'a
kehe ko he fiu faugata'a aupito ha e
Movete ae kakai kae osi kuo finangalo
o Sisu ke tau taha pe kora 'eku 'ou kole
atu kia Koe mo Sioa ke oua temou
toe fetu'utaki mai kia Ului 'o kau maia

Document 9.

Notes

1. Bulu, Joel. *An Autobiography.* (London, Wesleyan Mission House, 1871. Republished Nuku'alofa, Friendly Islands Bookshop and Taulua Press, 1993). p7.
2. Ibid.
3. Edwards, Ernie. *Rewiti: The Life and Work of E.H. Edwards.* (Wanganui, Maori Postal Sunday School, 1990). pp55,56.
4. Ibid. p65.
5. Dr Vautier's personal report in *The Treasury*, NZ Brethren Missionary Magazine, 1969.
6. GLO – Gospel Literature Outreach, a mission strategy developed by Colin Tilsley in the 1970s. It involved training in evangelism and discipleship followed by short-term visits to countries open to the gospel.
7. Foster Crane's personal report for Gospel Workers' and Elders' Conference, New Zealand, 1971.
8. Minutes of Tonga Gospel Fellowship, Chairman's Annual Report, 26 June 1973.
9. Ibid.
10. Dr Wilson was a stickler about meeting procedures, but this was an entirely foreign concept to a Tongan way of decision-making.
11. "Down in the valley with my Saviour I would go." William Cushing, 1878.
12. New Zealand was the birthplace of Every Boy's and Every Girl's Rallies in 1944. Rally is a church-based, uniformed organisation for children and young people from the ages of four to 18.

13. Molokau – *Scolopendra subspinipes* found throughout the Pacific. A very painful bite that can be lethal to infants.
14. Rev Shirley Waldemar Baker (1836-1903) was a Methodist missionary, adviser to George Tupou I, who loved these small bananas, sometimes also called "Lady's Fingers".
15. Attributed to Minnie E. Paull, 1897. In some versions the poem carries the supposedly Saxon title and refrain, "Doe ye nexte thynge."
16. Author's recording, 12/2/22.
17. The song "In Christ Alone My Hope is Found" is by Keith Getty and Stuart Townsend.
18. Recording of Inoke Feki testimony, 10 May 2022.
19. Niumeitolu, Heneli Taliai. *The State and the Church, the State of the Church in Tonga*. (Edinburgh, The University of Edinburgh, 2007).
20. *Matangi Tonga*, 2010. pacific.scoop.co.nz/2010/02/tongan-philosopher-futa-helu-dies-leaving-pacific-wide-legacy/
21. *Fakaafe* literally means "invitation". But this use refers specifically to a Sunday feast put on by one or a group of families.
22. *Umu* is a Tongan underground cooking method, as Māori hangi.
23. Kaeppler, Adrienne L. and Love, J.W. *The Garland Encyclocpedia of World Music*. Volume 1. (1998).
24. catalogue.nla.gov.au/Record/3017820/Details?lookfor=tohi&max=153&offset=87
25. Kiwi Ranch was a significant camping ministry in Rotorua, 1965-2010. Founded by Colleen's father and mother, Ces and Mavis Hilton. It now operates as Lakes Ranch.
26. Matt Redman. The song dates back to the late 1990s, born from a period of apathy within Matt's home church in England. "There was a dynamic missing, so the pastor did a pretty brave thing," he recalled in a BBC Radio interview. "He decided to get rid of the sound system and band for a season, and we gathered together with just our voices. His point was that we'd lost our way in worship, and the way to get back to the heart would be to strip everything away." Matt says the question initially led to some embarrassing silence,

but eventually people broke into a cappella songs and heartfelt prayers, encountering God in a fresh way.
27. As reported by Mele and Vaisioa Toulini.
28. *Misinale*: An annual missionary offering expected to be made by families within a village church. It was meant to be an expression of one's growing faith, but tradition turned it, in many instances, into competition with other families, even to relying on the missionary offering to make one fit for heaven.
29. Catechism teaching is a summary of the principles of the Christian faith in the form of questions and answers, used for religious instruction.
30. Elder Pita Hopoate was a passenger on the plane and has written an eyewitness report of the tragedy. www.churchofjesuschrist.org/study/ensign/2002/01/crash-landing
31. Twenty traditional noble titles were established by Siaosi Tupou I. Each were allotted an estate. In the modern Kingdom of Tonga there are 33 nobles with allotments. en.wikipedia.org/wiki/Tongan_nobles
32. nla.gov.au/nla.obj-341967135/view?sectionId=nla.obj-345548470&partId=nla.obj-341995353#page/n66/mode/1up
33. Augustus Toplady (1740-1788). The first stanza appeared in public in 1775 in a periodical called *The Gospel Magazine*. www.challies.com/hymn-stories/hymn-stories-rock-of-ages/
34. Edwards, Ernie. *Rewiti*. p65.
35. For an in-depth understanding of relationships between a para-church organisation and a major denomination read: www.academia.edu/28772732/KO_E_MOTU
36. Composed by Kirk Talley, 1982.
37. www.orthoreach.org.au/wp-content/uploads/2014/10/2013-Annual-Report-Orthopaedic-Outreach.pdf
38. A copy of the letter is included in the appendices.
39. For an indepth treatment of the relationship between churches involved in mission see Hitchen, John M., "Autonomy and Interdependence: Clarifying Biblical Patterns of Local Church

Relationships", a discussion paper for Christian Community Churches in New Zealand Conference, Eastern Beach, Auckland, 2017.
40. gc3.rocketspark.co.nz/blog/post/42031/Is-God-Calling-You/
41. Indices of the Tonga Gospel Church Constitution.
42. Burt, David. *Light on the Path*. (Auckland, Castle Publishing, 2013).

Bibliography

Crane, Foster. *Pilgrimage of Faith*. (Tauranga, Print Centre, 1984).

Edwards, Ernie. *Rewiti: The Life and Work of E.H. Edwards*. (Wanganui, Maori Postal Sunday School, 1990).

Pulu, Sioeli. *The Autobiography of a Native Minister in the South Seas*. (London, Wesleyan Mission House, 1871).

Reeson, Margaret. *Currency Lass*. (Sutherland, Albatross Books, 1985).

Thomas, John. *A History of Tonga*. (Seoul, Bible Society in Korea, 2013).

Niumeitolu, Heneli Taliai. *The State and the Church, the State of the Church in Tonga*. (Edinburgh, The University of Edinburgh, 2007).

Copyrights

Unless otherwise stated, scripture quotations are from The Holy Bible, English Standard Version. Other versions used as follows:

Scripture quotations marked (KJV) are taken from The Authorised (King James) Version. Rights in the Authorised Version in the United Kingdom are vested in the Crown. Reproduced by permission of the Crown's patentee, Cambridge University Press.

Scripture quotations marked (NET) are from the NET Bible® copyright ©1996, 2019 used with permission from Biblical Studies Press, L.L.C. All rights reserved.

Scripture quotations marked (NIV) are taken from the Holy Bible, New International Version®, NIV®. Copyright © 1973, 1978, 1984, 2011 by Biblica, Inc.™ Used by permission of Zondervan. All rights reserved worldwide.

Scripture quotations marked (NASB) are taken from the New American Standard Bible®, Copyright © 1960, 1971, 1977, 1995, 2020 by The Lockman Foundation. Used by permission. All rights reserved.

The maps on pages 17 and 182 are copyright © WorldAtlas.com. Used by permission.

The map on page 194 is by Saqib Qayyum. Licensed under Creative Commons Attribution-Share Alike. commons.wikimedia.org/wiki/File:Vava'u_travel_map.png

'E Sīsū, na'a ke tuku atu,
Mo kouna ho'o kau faifekau,
Ke fai he potu fuli pē
'A e misinale laumālie

'E Sīsū, 'omi ke mau 'ofa
Si'i fanga sipi mate noa:
Toe fai mai ho'o angi ē
"Mou misinale laumālie".

For an English translation of this hymn,
visit www.traditionalmusic.co.uk/sacred-songs/
assembled-at-thy-great-command-before-thy-face.htm

www.ingramcontent.com/pod-product-compliance
Lightning Source LLC
Chambersburg PA
CBHW062032290426
44109CB00026B/2601